A Memoir of Tōru Takemitsu

by **Asaka Takemitsu**
interviewed by Tetsuo O'hara

translated by
Tomoko Isshiki
with David Pacun and Mitsuko Ono

with a Foreword by Maki Takemitsu

iUniverse, Inc.
Bloomington

A Memoir of Tōru Takemitsu

iUniverse books may be ordered through booksellers or by contacting:

iUniverse
1663 Liberty Drive
Bloomington, IN 47403
www.iuniverse.com
1-800-Authors (1-800-288-4677)

Because of the dynamic nature of the Internet, any Web addresses or links contained in this book may have changed since publication and may no longer be valid. The views expressed in this work are solely those of the author and do not necessarily reflect the views of the publisher, and the publisher hereby disclaims any responsibility for them.

ISBN: 978-1-4502-7111-0 (sc)
ISBN: 978-1-4502-7112-7 (ebook)
ISBN: 978-1-4502-7113-4 (dj)

Printed in the United States of America

iUniverse rev. date: 11/30/2010

Contents

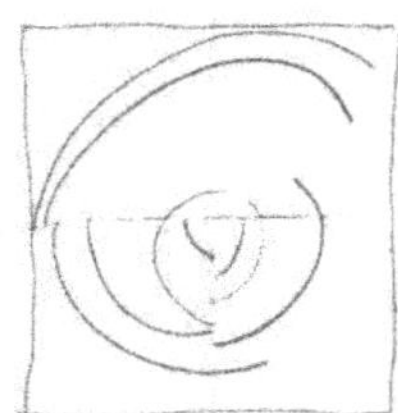

Chapter 4 Passion for Movies

Chapter 5   Daily life of a composer

Chapter 6 Music through Friendship

Acknowledgements

First and foremost, I would like to express my utmost respect and sincerest appreciation for Dr. David Pacun and Ms. Mitsuko Ono. Dr. Pacun, Associate Professor at Ithaca College, has assisted me with the revision of the text, and has also shared his insights based on his expertise and passion for the Japanese music. As the translation author of Peter Burt's *The Music of Tōru Takemitsu* and a co-editor of *Complete Takemitsu Edition*, Ms. Ono has served as a primary contact person for Ms. Asaka Takemitsu and other important sources in Japan, and has also provided Takemitsu's revised chronology for this book. Without their selfless dedication and tireless efforts, this project could not have come to fruition.

I would also like to extend my heartfelt gratitude to Mr. Tetsuo O'hara and Motoko Toi of Shōgakukan Publishing Company for their patience in dealing with the complexity of the copyright issues as well as for obtaining a set of Tōru Takemitsu's precious photos, making this book even more flavorful.

Last but not least, I would like to thank Ms. Asaka Takemitsu for giving me this wonderful opportunity to translate a truly fascinating story of one of the greatest composers of our time.

October, 2010

Tomoko Isshiki

Foreword

Tōru as my father, as my friend

It has been almost fourteen years since my father has passed. It has gone by in what seems like a flash, but still feels like a long time. When my father was alive, I was not interested in his work at all. Especially after I left the house in my late twenties, I hardly attended his concerts. To tell you the truth, I had little interest in classical music including contemporary music. My father understood my personality very well, so he tried to entice me with food when he asked me to go to his concerts. He would say, "We will go to eat Italian after the concert, so why don't you come?" or "Tonight we will go for Korean Barbeque!" When I still didn't show up for dinner after the concert, he called me up from the pub at midnight and said, "We are drinking with everyone, so can you come now?" I liked to drink with my father and talk about movies and music (not classical), so I went out for a drink with him often. And when I was drinking quickly, just like my father, he would always say to me, "Don't drink too much. Why is a young girl like you out drinking so late? You need to live more seriously." Well, he was the one who asked me to come along at midnight…

When I talk about my father to people who never knew him, most of them find it surprising. For people who only know 'composer, Tōru Takemitsu' from his music and essays, their image of my father is of someone who liked to be in nature and always listened to the sounds of the wind and of bird calls, an aloof person removed from the concerns of daily life, one who grimaced while being entirely absorbed in composition. Of course, he did have that side of him, but the father I knew had a different side. He liked the neon-lit streets of the city as much as he liked nature. He didn't mind solitude, but enjoyed being with his friends even more. He could be stubborn and difficult, but was also simple-minded and easily carried away. He was humorous and also very romantic. He was very human and tried to be a domestic man before he was a composer. He did his job as a composer in a very normal, everyday environment. At least it seemed like that to me.

My father was an early-riser, took a long bath, had a big breakfast, and chatted endlessly with my mother. Then, as if they hadn't chatted enough, he said, "Well, I guess I better start working" and went into his study. When he came out for lunch and found that the meal was one of his favorites, such as fried noodle or udon, he would leap for joy like a child. In his late years, he didn't work much at night, but rather he enjoyed watching baseball games on TV or listened to them on the radio. In the off-season, we rented videos and watched movies together. Anyway, it was a very lively home.

After my father's death, I became more inclined to go to concerts, and am now involved in work related to classical music. This is mainly because my father was a musician and had many friends and acquaintances in the field of music. I myself have little knowledge of music and I wonder why it turned out this way. As the daughter of Tōru Takemitsu, I can say that my life with him was really fun. In choosing my current profession, I realize that his memory is not fading in time but is still strongly present with me. I wonder how he thinks of me from the other world. I am looking forward to seeing his reaction when I join him at the pub in heaven.

October, 2010

Maki Takemitsu

Introduction

Tōru Takemitsu (1930-1996) was the first Japanese composer to receive international recognition in the field of classical music, and is now widely regarded as one of the greatest composers of the late 20th century. Largely self-taught, Takemitsu created his own unique sound world, one not bound by convention, but incorporating ideas from nature, everyday life, and other art forms. Takemitsu rose to prominence in 1957 when Igor Stravinsky praised his *Requiem for Strings*, and later gained critical acclaim for his 1967 masterpiece, *November Steps*, which pitted Japanese traditional instruments against the Western orchestra. Though best known in the West for his concert music, Takemitsu was also a master composer of music for film, TV, theater, and radio drama.

To date, many books and studies have been written on Takemitsu, and Takemitsu's own writings and conversation books (many undertaken in conjunction with other artists) have been issued. One of the most important recent publications, however, is the *Complete Takemitsu Edition*, issued in Japan by Shōgakukan between 2002 and 2004. This edition contains recordings of Takemitsu's entire output of concert music, extant movie scores, TV, radio and theater works, and electronic and tapes pieces—all told, fifty-five CDs organized into five volumes. Many of Takemitsu's unpublished works and early study pieces were newly recorded for this edition, and each volume was accompanied by a separate book containing extensive program notes and reviews, additional commentary and essays, and interviews by editor-in-chief Tetsuo O'hara with Takemitsu's close friends and acquaintances, including Takemitsu's wife, Asaka Takemitsu (*nee* Wakayama). Originally issued in newsletters appended to each volume, Shōgakukan later gathered the O'hara/ Asaka-san interviews into an independent book,

Sakkyokuka, Takemitsu Tōru tono Hibi wo Kataru (Tōkyō: 2006). It is this book that is the source of the present manuscript.

In all, O'hara interviewed Asaka Takemitsu six-times between 2002 and 2004, yielding over twenty hours of material. As a special supplement to this English edition, Mitsuko Ono, a Takemitsu specialist and editor of *Complete Takemitsu Edition*, conducted a new interview with Mrs. Takemitsu in May 2010; this new interview is included here as Chapter 6. As a friend, lover, and wife to Takemitsu, Asaka-san was initially hesitant to talk about her late husband, but quickly warmed to the task, unveiling valuable new information about the composer's life and his compositional processes, the difficult period after the war and the subsequent postwar art movement in Japan, Takemitsu's friends, his love for movies, his daily routines, and his final days. In her candid and outspoken words, Asaka relates that "Tōru-san was the happiest when he was composing."

One significant early event, not included in the interviews, is worth mention. Before meeting Asaka Wakayama in his late teens, Takemitsu already had determined to become a composer, but he had no means to carry out his goal. Japan was undergoing a tough period following the war, and Takemitsu's poverty during his early life was no exception. The readers might find it strange, then, for a young boy, one without any musical training and who lived on the margins of society, to dream of becoming a composer. Later in life, Takemitsu repeatedly recounted this incident in various interviews and in his essays.

> Two months before the war ended, the fifteen-year-old
> Takemitsu was forced to work at a military provisions
> base in the mountains in Saitama prefecture. It was a
> bitter experience for him, but it was in those extreme
> circumstances that he decided to become a composer.
> Although listening to foreign music was prohibited and
> those in camp were only allowed to sing military songs,
> one day in an underground dugout, a cadet secretly let
> him and other interns listen to the French chanson *Parlez-*

moi d'amour by Lucienne Boyer on a wind-up gramophone. While other interns were amused by this forbidden music, it came as an enormous shock to the young impressionable Takemitsu. As he described later, "I didn't know this kind of sweet and beautiful music existed. It felt as if electricity has gone through my body, and my whole flesh and blood had become totally enthralled with that music. That was when I decided that I wanted to 'be in music' once the war was over."

But achieving this dream was not a foregone conclusion. After the war had ended, Takemitsu's family moved to Asaka's neighborhood, and Takemitsu earned money selling cigarettes and gum on the black market, and eventually finding work as a 'band boy' at an American military base in Yokohama. Given access to the facilities during the day, Takemitsu taught himself to play piano and also learned English. Still, when he was sixteen, Takemitsu showed signs of tuberculosis and was eventually hospitalized in 1953. Asaka, who also shared the same illness, though to less serious degree, cared for him at the hospital, and following Takemitsu's release in 1954, the couple started to live together. In these interviews, Asaka relates how, even in the depth of poverty and illness after the war, Takemitsu never gave up on being a composer and always remained optimistic; she highlights how Tōru owed so much of his success to those people who helped him; he indeed had many friends. This volume is, perhaps more than anything else, a testament to Takemitsu's wonderful friendship with composers, artists, writers, and performers with whom he came into contact throughout his life.

Tomoko Isshiki

Tetsuo O'hara and Asaka Takemitsu

*Notes on Japanese words

Diacritical marks have been used in this book to describe Japanese pronunciation on long vowel sounds such as; "Toru" as "Tōru"; "Tokyo" as "Tōkyō."
Conventionally, the movie and TV titles list in Japanese title followed by English translation title, however, this book lists reversed for readability reasons.
Names are given following English conventions with the sir name last.

Chapter 1

The Encounter

This interview covers Asaka's early years with Takemitsu—how they first met, their respective battles with tuberculosis (a disease that reached nearly epidemic proportions in Japan), then the first years of their marriage in Senzoku-Ike (a town favored by members of the NHK Symphony Orchestra) and Takemitsu's first work for NHK Radio. Near the conclusion Asaka recounts several famous episodes in Takemitsu's life—the piano sent by Mayuzumi as a gift, Takemitsu's meeting with Stravinsky, and his friendship with art critic Shūzō Takiguchi, one of many vital interactions that Takemitsu had with people outside of music. The interview begins on what may be a quintessentially Japanese note, namely the precise manner in which people address one another.

Takemitsu's own illustration

First meeting with Tōru

Tetsuo O'hara: Because Shuntarō Tanikawa[1] and others call you "Asaka-san," it wasn't long before I started calling you "Asaka-san" too. [*laughs*] And you called Mr. Takemitsu "Tōru-san." Have you always called him that way?

Asaka Takemitsu: I don't remember what I called him at first. Long before our marriage I used to call him "Tōru-san." We called each other "Tōru-san" and "Asaka-san" all the time. Even my daughter Maki started calling him "Tōru-san" after she grew up—probably because I referred to him in that way. [*laughs*]

O: Well then, "Asaka-san," I would like to ask you many questions. If you prefer to dodge any questions, just let me know. [*laughs*] So to begin, how did you first meet Takemitsu? How old were you?

T: We first met in 1951. I had just graduated from school, so I was twenty-one years old. Tōru was my neighbor, and my younger brother was his friend.

O: How interesting. I thought you two met at the Shiki Theatre Company[2] through his work. Where did you live at that time?

T: The neighborhood is Setagaya-Daita[3] in Setagaya-ward, Tōkyō. It was called Setagaya-Nakahara when I was a child.

O: Which part of Setagaya-Daita?

---

[1] Shuntarō Tanikawa (1931-): a renowned poet and translator, and one of Takemitsu's closest friends. Takemitsu used Tanikawa's poems in *Family Tree* (1992), *Grass* (1982), and *Vocalism A·I* (1956).

[2] Shiki Theatre Company: established in 1953, it became the largest and most successful theater company in Japan. Asaka-san appeared in their second production, a French version of *Antigone*. Takemitsu first worked with Shiki in 1955, taking charge of the music for a production of Anouilh's *La Sauvage*.

[3] Setagaya-Daita: in Setagaya ward, Tōkyō. It takes twelve minutes from Shinjuku by Odakyū Train Line.

T: It was a five or six-minute walk from the station. There used to be a river there—now it's a culvert—and my family lived in front of it.

O: Was it on the west side, facing toward Shinjuku? Didn't that area suffer from war damage?

T: Yes, it was on the west side. That part of town used to be a residential area before the war, and I had lived there before entering elementary school. When the war became severe, my family evacuated to Shikoku,[1] and when that area became dangerous, they moved to my father's hometown in Mie prefecture[2] in the mountains. But I, for the life of me, didn't want to leave Tōkyō at all. My sister and her husband had rented a house near where my parents lived after they were married. So I stayed at my sister's house and attended an all-girls' school from there. There were some houses in my neighborhood that suffered damages, but fortunately, my sister's house survived. After the war, my whole family returned to Tōkyō, and we all lived together in that tiny house.

O: Right after the war was a period when the entire family lined up futons and slept together in one room, some as small as six *tatami* mats.[3]

T: Yes, everyone lived like that. My sister's house had only four small rooms, and my whole family lived together.

O: And your sister's house was close to Takemitsu's house?

T: Tōru's family—along with another family—lived across the street about five houses down from my sister's house. They had moved to their friend's house in our neighborhood after losing their own home to war damage. The area beyond their friend's house had burned down… In those days you were lucky if you had a place to live. Many people were burned out of their homes, and ended up with nowhere to stay. Some lived in dugout shelters with roofs made from iron sheeting. During the air raids, many incendiary bombs were dropped on that area.

---

[1] Shikoku: the smallest of Japan's four main islands.
[2] Mie prefecture: part of the Kansai region, it is located about forty miles from Ōsaka.
[3] *Tatami*: traditional mats woven of rice straw. A six-mat room will measure roughly 9x12 feet.

O: It is hard to imagine today…

T: There was a house with a very nice black fence near where I grew up. The poet Sakutarō Hagiwara[4] lived there, as I think his own house had burnt down too. Tōru's family was burned out twice before they moved to the house in my area, so they have no photos of that time. Until then, Tōru lived with his aunt and not so much with his own family. But finally, at the house in Setagaya-Daita, he was reunited with his mother and younger sisters.

O: So, was that how he became friends with your younger brother?

T: Yes. They were about the same age, so they got to know each other and started to play together. Tōru also came over to our house to play.

O: What is the difference in age between you and Takemitsu?

T: I am one year older than he is. My brother and I are two years apart, and Tōru is in the middle. I was born in February and Tōru in October, so I am older by one and a half years. After getting married, I would say, "We are one year apart in age" and he would say, "Aren't we two years apart?" In the old days, we used the East Asian age counting.[5] He didn't have to emphasize such a minor detail, don't you think? [*laughs*]

O: You're right. [*laughs*]

T: My brother became close to him, and they would go out to eat or out to swim in the Tama River during the summer. At that time, Tama was still clean. They would take the Odakyū Train Line to the Izumi-Tama River Station. Young people in our neighborhood gathered and formed an *a cappella* chorus. We said 'chorus' but we didn't have that many members, maybe about ten people altogether. Tōru joined the group and conducted too.

---

[4] Sakutarō Hagiwara (1886-1942): Japanese poet who established colloquial Japanese free verse. He was among the first poets who broke the traditional, metered forms.
[5] In this old system, years were added with each Lunar New Year (not each birthday) and everyone turned a year older at the same time. In Japan, babies are said to be one year old at birth.

Asaka and Tōru in Kamakura, 1960.

O: Takemitsu conducted?

T: Yes. Once, when we were singing some trivial song, he said, "Let's sing this one" and began to conduct "My Bonnie Lies Over the Ocean." At that time, Tōru and I didn't really know each other. He didn't care about his appearance at all—his pants had holes in the knees and were sewn together like a swab, and he wore women's *geta*[6] with red straps. One time, he put on an American Army uniform and we all frowned at him. [*laughs*]

O: Do you think the uniform was an old one from the United States occupying forces?

T: He was employed at the army base in Camp Zama, so maybe it was. He worked as a 'band boy'[7] at night and was able to use the piano during the day in return.

O: Was it around this time that he made a portable keyboard by drawing a piano on a cardboard? Did you ever see it?

T: I never saw it, but he did tell me about it.

O: I heard that, while you were in school, you were involved in a theatrical club.

T: When I was twenty-years old, I became involved in theatrical acting with a friend who also went to the Keisen Girls School[8] in which I was enrolled. We didn't have anywhere to practice, so I, along with three members of the Tōkyō University drama club, read scripts on the lawn at the Meiji Shrine. One of them knew an actor called Tomoo Nagai and I consulted him several times. He told me to audition for Haiyūza[9] Actors Studio, so I did. But at the final stage of the audition, they took an X-ray for the medical exam, and that is when I discovered that I had

---

[6] *Geta*: Japanese wooden clogs.
[7] 'Band boy': an equivalent of 'roadie.'
[8] Keisen Girls School: a private Christian girl's school established in 1929.
[9] Haiyūza Theatre Company: established in 1944. It continues to present Japanese versions of realist Western dramas. Haiyūza Actors Studio is their subsidiary.

tuberculosis. Mr. Nagai told me to take a leave of absence from the acting studio, but I couldn't do it. I was in deep shock, and thought there was no way I could pull myself together again. Staying in good health had been one thing that I prided on as a child, and I was the only one of my five siblings who never got sick. Anyway, I just wanted to focus on curing this illness. So I went to the Anti-Tuberculosis Association in Suidōbashi, Tōkyō and took the pneumothorax treatment.

O: What kind of treatment was that?

T: Fortunately, my tuberculosis was not that serious, but there was a shadow on my left pulmonary apex. They didn't have chemotherapy back then. Pumping air into the pleura[10] restrained the activity in the lung and stopped the shadow from spreading. I went for treatment twice a week. Since they put air into the pleura and shrank the lung, my breathing became labored and I had such a difficult time breathing on my way home. Eventually the air naturally leaked out, so I would go back for another treatment. They took an X-ray to see how much air had leaked, and next injected more air into the pleura with a big fat needle, like the ones they use to sew *tatami*. And then they would take another X-ray to check whether or not the air went in properly. I did that for four years. I'm surprised I didn't develop cancer from all the X-rays. [*laughs*]

O: Was it after this period of your own illness that Takemitsu also developed tuberculosis?[11]

T: My brother said, "We went swimming at Tama River and Tōru spat blood. It was bloody phlegm." So I brought Tōru to the Anti-Tuberculosis Association. We found out that there were big holes on both sides of his lung. The doctor said, "If it continues like this, you won't live long. You need to start treatment immediately." So we discussed it with Tōru's mother, and decided to hospitalize him at Keiō Hospital.[12] His mother worked at Yasuda Fire Insurance Company (currently called Sompo Japan Insurance) and it helped that they had

---

[10] Pleura: The thin layer of tissue that covers and protects the lungs.
[11] Tuberculosis was the leading cause of death in Japan in the first half of the 20th-century. There were fears that it would become a national epidemic.
[12] Takemitsu was hospitalized from June 1953 until March 1954.

good medical benefits. That was in 1953, one year before we started living together. I read a lot of books about tuberculosis, so I was pretty knowledgeable about this illness. But Tōru was totally indifferent.

O: You were firm and strong.

T: In that respect, yes.

O: Did Takemitsu recover after that?

T: When he was hospitalized, they treated him using three antibiotics together: Streptomycin, PAS, and Isonicotinic acid hydrazide. And these treatments worked really well for Tōru. Many people complained of upset stomach from PAS, but his stomach was strong. The shadow in his lung started to shrink after taking a lot of PAS. But even before he was completely cured, Tōru desperately wanted to go home. His first two pieces—*Lento in Due Movimenti* (1950)[13] and *Distance de Fée* (1951)—had been premiered, but he wasn't confident that he could make it as a composer. He had no money either. So even though he was still in the hospital, he would go to conduct his own music live on NHK Radio[14] wearing a cardigan over his pajamas.

O: So, this incident was after *Jikken Kōbō*[15] ('Experimental Workshop') was formed in 1951.

T: Yes, it was about two years later. He participated in *Jikken Kōbō* but wasn't so active in it as of yet. Most of his friends were in better financial shape than him; I would say that, in those days, musicians tended to come from wealthy families. Tōru had the passion to become a composer but didn't even own a piano. Right after his music started being performed, he was hospitalized with tuberculosis, so I think he became frustrated. Even though he was still ill, Tōru wouldn't budge and

---

[13] *Lento in Due Movimenti* was premiered on Dec. 7th 1950 at the seventh *Shin-Sakkyokuha Kyōkai* recital.

[14] NHK: *Nippon Hōsō Kyōkai* ('Japan Broadcasting Corporation') is Japan's national public broadcaster.

[15] *Jikken Kōbō*: a multidisciplinary art group led by Shūzō Takiguchi. It explored new directions in the arts and introduced avant-garde works from Japan and abroad. Takemitsu was one of the founding members.

he said, "I am leaving the hospital no matter what." But his mother told him to stay until he was completely cured. He had two younger sisters, and other families lived in the same house. So it was impossible to take him back home until his tuberculosis was gone. Tōru's mother was working full-time, which was uncommon back then, having been widowed when Tōru was seven years old. In such circumstances, a mother will usually want her first son to find a decent job and earn money for the family, but Tōru wanted to become a composer even though he had no music degree. I think she was surprised, but she didn't oppose to it. Instead she said, "I won't look after you. If you can do it by yourself, then it's fine. Go ahead."

O: Maybe Tōru's mother wasn't worried because you were there for him.

T: When Tōru was hospitalized, his mother bought me a commuter pass for the train and asked me to visit the hospital everyday. Only I couldn't go everyday. I had to work and make a living myself. [*laughs*] And then Tōru insisted upon leaving the hospital. So I thought I had to take him in. [*laughs*]

O: What were you doing at that time?

T: After I found out that I had tuberculosis, I almost gave up acting. I was working during the day and rehearsing with a theater group called *Geijutsu Kyōkai* ('Art Association') at night. This group stayed together for two years and later on formed the puppet theater group *Kakashiza*. Eventually I joined the Shiki Theatre Company. Around the same time, my brother moved to the Ōsaka area and my parents went with him, so I lived alone in a boarding house in Gōtokuji,[16] Tōkyō. It was such a small room and I also had to think about taking care of Tōru. [*laughs*] I joined the Shiki Theatre Company and performed a bit, but realized I am not suited for acting. Tōru said he couldn't bare to watch me act. So I left the company in 1953.

O: Then, you started to live together…

---

[16] Gōtokuji: in Setagaya ward, Tōkyō. It takes three minutes from Setagaya-Daita by train.

Members of Jikken Kōbō on a trip to Nasu Heights.
From Left: Hiroyoshi Suzuki, Kiyoji Ōtsuji, Shōzō Kitadai, Tōru Takemitsu, Kazuo Fukushima, Asaka Takemitsu, Hideko Fukushima, Makoto Kitadai, and Mrs. Kitadai. In the car from left, Jōji Yuasa and Kuniharu Akiyama. ca. 1957.   photo© Kiyoji Ōtsuji

T: Tōru and I started living together in 1954. Hideko Fukushima of *Jikken Kōbo* helped us find a rental house in Senzoku-Ike,[17] Tōkyō. We lived in a two-room apartment on the second floor of a small house, and I think the rent was five thousand yen. So it wasn't a fancy marriage or anything, but our friends brought us gifts on June 15th and celebrated with us. I had some household belongings from my single days in Tōkyō. But Tōru, as the groom, moved in with nothing but a cardboard box full of music, and some other stuff. [*laughs*] He felt sorry for me and brought one beautifully varnished *hibachi*[18] from his house. Tōru wore *geta* and had nothing proper to wear. I complained that he couldn't visit NHK or anywhere looking like that, so my brother took pity on him and got him a navy blue suit from somewhere. In high school in those days, people

---

[17] Senzoku-Ike: in Ōta Ward, Tōkyō. It takes about forty minutes from Setagaya-Daita by train.
[18] *Hibachi*: a porcelain charcoal stove.

bartered one thing for another or exchanged goods for rice. Tōru wore that blue suit for a long time, and it was miserable…[*laughs*] Of course, my parents opposed our marriage, but being unable to stand by any longer, I took custody of him. [*laughs*] He was ill, and didn't know whether he could make it as a composer. But I didn't think about the future.

O: You said you couldn't stand by any longer, but had you listened to Takemitsu's compositions already?

T: Before we got married, he gave me a concert ticket and asked me to come, so I went with my elder sister. The piece—*Lento in Due Movimenti* for solo piano—was his very first premiere. I also went to hear *Distance de Fée* for violin and piano performed by violinist Akiko Suwa. By that time, I was familiar with the members of *Jikken Kōbō*, but I never really thought about whether Tōru could be successful as a composer. *Lento in Due Movimenti* and *Distance de Fée* were so different from the music I had heard before, and I didn't know if they were any good. But I guess I did feel he had something special. Members of *Jikken Kōbō* got along well together and visited each others' houses frequently, and quite often I was invited to go along. I felt that everyone found him difficult to deal with. Tōru was not healthy, had no money, and used to disappear suddenly. One time, everybody got so worried and searched for him, only to find out later that he had taken a train by himself as far as Kōriyama[19] to visit Jōji Yuasa's[20] house. Mr. Yuasa's father was a medical doctor. Other times, and without any hesitation, Tōru would spend the night under the eaves of somebody's house. [*laughs*]

O: That is troublesome. [*laughs*]

T: I remember one time he suddenly came over to my house in the middle of the night. There was no TV, so most households went to bed before midnight. But he came over after midnight and slid open the entrance door of our house. My father got mad and yelled at him, "Tōru-

---

[19] Kōriyama: in Fukushima prefecture, north of Tōkyō. It takes about five hours from Tōkyō by train.
[20] Jōji Yuasa (1929-): renowned Japanese composer. He was a founding member of *Jikken Kōbō* and maintained a long lasting relationship with Takemitsu.

san! What time do you think it is?!" [*laughs*] He didn't have a sense of time or any common sense, and was eccentric in a way. My brother did get along well with him, but one time they had a big fight. My brother was sleeping in the middle of the night, and Tōru asked him, "Shigeto-san, let's go to eat *ramen* in Shimo-Kitazawa." *Ramen* wasn't that fancy a thing but everybody was hungry in those days, so my brother was happy and said, "OK, let's go. Can you wait a minute?" So he changed his clothes and went outside. Then Tōru said, "I'm not going." He had changed his mind while my brother was changing his clothes. My brother was normally calm and didn't get angry easily, but this time he got really mad at him and yelled, "What?!" and grabbed Tōru's collar and started to fight. [*laughs*]

O: I don't blame your brother for getting mad!

T: Tōru was really strange. Another time, he suddenly came to my house in the middle of the night and just sat in the parlor; he didn't speak at all and stayed still for a long time. Then he suddenly murmured, "A moth!" I really don't know what he was thinking. Anyway, he was a little odd. Now that I look back, maybe he was thinking about music all the time and wasn't interested in anything else. Then he was hospitalized with tuberculosis, got discharged, and started to live with me. I heard that everyone was relieved and expressed their thanks to me. [*laughs*]

O: It seems to me that Takemitsu became less audacious as he got older, didn't he?

T: Yes, he became too decent. [*laughs*] He wasn't the artist type who, like, suddenly hits upon an idea and writes it down. Instead, he had fun with his work and kept regular hours like an office worker: wake up in the morning, compose, eat breakfast, compose again. In the case of film music or radio drama music, he had deadlines so he would stay up all night. But, after he woke up the next morning he said he could not trust the work he did the night before. He would get too self-absorbed and carried away, so he said it's not good to work at night. Many people expressed their concern for me and said, "It must be difficult for your family to have a husband who is composing at home." But he was happy if I served him meals and filled his teacup when he was composing, so he wasn't a difficult person.

O: So the reckless behavior of his youth gradually faded away.

T: Yes, Kuniharu Akiyama[21] told me that Takemitsu became a little boring after meeting Shuntarō Tanikawa and me. Mr. Tanikawa is a poet but he had common sense; and I grew up in a normal family, so I had common sense too. He said if Tōru hadn't met the two of us, then his wild and reckless side might not have been lost, and he could have written more interesting pieces and lived more like a daredevil. But if I didn't exist, he would have died sooner. If he didn't have anyone to say, "Too many cigarettes, too much drinking, go to sleep now!"—and I admit that I might have been a little annoying—what might have happened to him? I'm giving myself a round of applause for that. [*laughs*]

In Senzoku-Ike

O: Can you tell us about the time when you lived in Senzoku-Ike? You had just married, correct?

T: The house in Senzoku-Ike had only two rooms, a six-mat room and four and a half-mat room. The six-mat room was in a Western style and the four and a half-mat room was in a Japanese style. We lived on the second floor of a cottage, separate from the main house, which was owned by a carpenter who had built the house for his own future marriage. The carpenter was still single then and lived alone in the main house, so I could use the cottage's downstairs kitchen all by myself. A few months after moving there, I began to vomit blood. I tried chemotherapy for the first time, and it worked pretty well. At that time, many orchestral members in the NHK Symphony lived in the Senzoku-Ike area. Senzoku-Ike was called 'NHK Symphony village.' Our next-door neighbor, Heihachirō Mita, was a bassoonist in the NHK Symphony. When we lived in Senzoku-Ike, it was like we were under the care of Mr. Mita's family. Almost everyday, he would invite us,

---

21 Kuniharu Akiyama (1929-96): poet, music critic, producer, and founding member of *Jikken Kōbō*. Impressed with Takemitsu's debut piece, he (along with Jōji Yuasa) went backstage to meet Takemitsu after the concert.

"Takemitsu-chan! Dinner is ready!" We ate at their place quite frequently. They knew we had no money.

O: So that's why, in the mid-1950s, bassoon is often used in Takemitsu's compositions.

T: Yes. Mr. Mita and Tōru formed 'Group MT' and encouraged each other to do more radio drama music at NHK. Tōru said, "This would be a good freelance job for Mita-san," and often composed music with bassoon in it.

O: That means that Takemitsu's music was broadcast on the radio quite frequently, correct?

T: Yes, it was. In those days *Children's Time*[22] and even dramatic productions were performed 'live.' It made for a tense atmosphere. Sound effects—ocean waves for instance—were made by shaking *azuki* beans in a bamboo box. It was totally different from nowadays.

O: Yes, in those days everything was broadcast live, including the background music and the sound effects.

T: One time, Mr. Mita introduced a very unusual instrument called the sarrusophone[23] to Tōru and demonstrated it for him. It had an interesting sound and Tōru used it in one of his compositions.

O: And that piece is *Indoor Concerto* (1955). I understand that a turning point in Takemitsu's work for NHK came when he began working with the noted producer Naoya Yoshida[24]?

T: Yes, I remember very clearly when Mr. Yoshida visited us in Senzoku-Ike. It was just after Tōru returned home from the hospital.

---

[22] A radio program for school children.
[23] Sarrusophone: a double-reed instrument used in military bands.
[24] Naoya Yoshida (1931-): Producer and writer at NHK. He collaborated with Takemitsu on many occasions, including historical TV drama *Yoshitsune Minamoto*.

O: Mr. Yoshida wanted to commission Fumio Hayasaka,[25] but Hayasaka said there is another good young composer and introduced him to Takemitsu.

T: Yes, yes. Actually, other people in the broadcast station were opposed to Takemitsu, saying that he was too young. But Mr. Yoshida recommended him strongly. Tōru undertook his first commission with Mr. Yoshida for NHK's special program *Four Seasons of Sound* ('Oto no Shiki' 1955). And after that, since Mr. Yoshida understood Tōru's way of doing things, he let him work freely. This was an important starting point for Tōru. If it wasn't for this, he could not have kept the same positive attitude when writing for radio or TV as he had when writing concert pieces.

O: Mr. Yoshida left a long legacy of broadcasts in collaboration with Takemitsu: *Japanese Crest Patterns* ('Nihon no Monyō' 1961), *Yoshitsune Minamoto* (1966), and *The Legend for the Future* ('Mirai e no Isan' 1974).

Piano sent from Mayuzumi

O: Wasn't it around the same time that a piano was sent to Takemitsu by Toshirō Mayuzumi?[26]

T: Yes, it was during this time in Senzoku-Ike. Suddenly a piano appeared by courier—it was from Mr. Mayuzumi. In those days, pianos were very precious. The only ones available were those that did not get burned during the war. So it was quite amazing that Mr. Mayuzumi would suddenly send a piano during such a tough period. After receiving the piano, Tōru reaffirmed his passion for composing music and said,

---

25 Fumio Hayasaka (1914-55): Japanese composer best known today for his film music. He scored Akira Kurosawa's *Rashōmon* (1950), *Ikiru* (1952); and Kenji Mizoguchi's *Ugetsu* (1954), *The Crucified Lovers* (1954). Takemitsu assisted Hayasaka on the score for *Rashōmon*.

26 Toshirō Mayuzumi (1929-97): one of Japan's most celebrated Japanese composers. His most important works include *Nirvana Symphony* (1958) and *Kinkakuji* (1976). He also hosted the TV program *Untitled Concert* ('Daimei no nai ongaku-kai' 1964-1997) and helped to introduce Western classical music to Japanese audiences.

"Now I am determined to make it as a composer. I cannot do it halfheartedly." He used to say, "I will always be indebted to Mayuzumi-san."[27]

O: How did Mayuzumi know that Takemitsu didn't have a piano?

T: Before meeting Mr. Mayuzumi, Tōru met Yasushi Akutagawa.[28] Mr. Akutagawa's first wife was a painter and Tōru knew her through *Jikken Kōbō*. Mr. Akutagawa went to Fumio Hayasaka's house often, so maybe they met each other there. One time, Tōru said really impertinent things to Mr. Akutagawa. Members of *Jikken Kōbō* used to get together and critique music and art. One day, they went to Hibiya-Kōkaidō Hall to hear Sadao Bekku's[29] concert and criticized his compositions, saying that they were boring. Tōru wore *geta* to the concert, which was inappropriate, and he made a rattling noise with them when the piece ended. Well, they were young. Still, afterwards, Tōru praised Mr. Bekku and said, "Bekku-san didn't let us down. It was well-written." [*laughs*] In those days, young people wanted to reject everything that already existed. After that incident, Mr. Akutagawa said, "Hey Takemitsu-san, before you quibble over someone else's music, write a decent piece. While you are chopping logic, why don't you write one decent piece yourself?" Tōru was offended, but he was roused to act by this occasion. Along with Ikuma Dan, Mr. Akutagawa, and Mr. Mayuzumi formed *San nin no kai* ('A group of three composers').[30] They had had flamboyant debuts as composers and were successful right from the start, whereas Tōru was ill and had no money. It was a time when Japanese films were still spending money on film music, and they also had many commissions from several movie studios. I heard that Mr. Akutagawa said to Mr. Mayuzumi, "There is an interesting young guy. I think he has talent, but no money and he doesn't even own a piano." After hearing that story, Mr. Mayuzumi sent his

---

[27] Literally: "I cannot sleep pointing my feet toward Mayuzumi-san."

[28] Yasushi Akutagawa (1925-89): Japanese composer and TV personality. He entered Soviet Union in 1954 illegally and made friends with Kabalevsky, Khachaturian, and Shostakovich. He is the great writer Ryūnosuke Akutagawa's third son.

[29] Sadao Bekku (1922-): Japanese composer. He studied with Darius Milhaud and Olivier Messiaen at the Paris Conservatory in the 1950s.

[30] *San nin no kai*: this group was responsible for many important premieres, including Akutagawa's *Ellora Symphony* (1958), Mayuzumi's *Nirvana Symphony* (1958), and Dan's *The Silk Road* (1955).

piano to Tōru.

O: I heard that Mayuzumi helped Takemitsu in various other ways…

T: I think Mr. Mayuzumi felt it was rude to just hand out money for nothing. Tōru was asked by Mr. Mayuzumi to help with his film scores, and went over to his house to work with him. While Tōru was having a hard time composing his part, he could hear a pencil running fast on the staff paper in the next room. He thought, "Wow, that's amazing. Actually Mayuzumi-san doesn't need my help. He can get it done by himself so easily." Still, Mr. Mayuzumi put some money in an envelope and gave it to Tōru upon leaving. One time when I picked him up, it started to rain. I was shabbily dressed and Yōko Katsuragi, Mayuzumi's wife and a famous actress herself, lent me a beautiful black raincoat with a small collar. I tried to returned to her, but she said, "Oh, don't worry. Please keep it." So I accepted her kindness and wore that jacket all the time. [*laughs*]

O: The piano from Mayuzumi is still at this villa in Miyota[31] where you live now. I saw it the other day, and was deeply moved.

T: Truly, it was an unforgettable act of kindness. When Tōru received the Suntory Music Award in 1991, Mr. Mayuzumi was the first to greet him at the ceremony, and Tōru told the audience the story of when the piano was sent to him. He started choking up and couldn't talk anymore. He just kept looking down. Everyone was so surprised and didn't know what to do. Then Mr. Mayuzumi said, "This story is told like a heroic tale, but in later years Takemitsu returned the money to me little by little. This side of the story hasn't been told, so I wanted to make it clear." It must have been a small amount of money though. When I look back on Tōru's life, he was so lucky to be surrounded by great people. That's why he was able to make it this far. Musicians and composers usually have rivalries, so it is hard for them to support each other like that.

---

[31] Miyota: in Kitasaku District, Nagano prefecture. It is located about five hours by train from Tōkyō.

The newlywed couple in Senzoku-Ike in front of the piano Mayuzumi sent as a gift.

O: The fact that Mayuzumi did so much for Takemitsu proves that he acknowledged his talent.

T: I don't know—probably he thought, "There is an interesting guy." Mr. Mayuzumi also went through hard times. When he was in college, he played jazz piano part-time in Yokohama. In those days, only a handful of musicians weren't poor or didn't have to go through hardships. It was a tough time for everybody. Mr. Akutagawa also went through a lot.

Requiem for Strings

O: You two moved to Kamakura out of concern for Takemitsu's health.

T: In Kamakura, we rented a cottage. Actually, Ikuma Dan had rented it earlier, and a composer named Tetsusaburō Hirai, who mainly wrote ballet music, lived there after him. Tōru composed his ballet score *A Trip on the Galactic Railway* ('Ginga Tetsudō no Tabi' 1953) for Akiko Tachibana Ballet Company, and Mr. Hirai conducted that piece. Mr. Hirai said, "If your body is weak, it's better to live where the air is good. Why don't you come to Kamakura?" In 1955, we moved to a place called Sasuke in Kamakura. We lived there for five years.

O: How was his health after moving to Kamakura?

T: Tuberculosis required staying rested, so he was in and out of bed. Due to being poor when we were young, perhaps his tuberculosis was not completely cured and sometimes it became worse. He was using three antibiotics together—Streptomycin, PAS, and Isonicotinic acid hydrazide—but gradually he developed resistance to these drugs and they became less effective. Later he used a new drug called Pyramide and that worked really well on him. We saw a good doctor who had opened a sanitarium not far from Kamakura. The doctor and the nurse were very good people, and we owe them a lot.

O: So you moved, but his condition didn't get much better...

T: There were times when he didn't even have the strength to hold his chopsticks, so I fed him by spoon, little by little. But when he was composing the radio drama *Flame* ('Honō') (1955), he stayed up late night after night at the studio, and he didn't come home for more than a month! I was so worried that his illness might return. I sometimes brought him food and drink just to see how he was doing. It was a tough time, and my role was to turn down commissions that came in. I always thought, "What if he becomes bedridden again?" Whenever he received a commission, he would ask me, "What do you think?" and I would say, "No, don't take it," then he was able to make up his mind to say no. But actually, it is scary to turn down a commission as a freelancer. If you reject a commission, maybe you won't get another offer; but if you do take it, you might have to stay up all night. In Tōru's case, I had a good excuse and could say that he could not overwork because of his health. As a result, he could select the work that he really wanted to do. So I think it turned out better in the long run. It would've been nice if we had had more money at that time, but it was just enough to make ends meet. We didn't eat out and nobody lived a luxurious life back then.

O: During those difficult times, physically and financially, Takemitsu composed *Requiem for Strings* (1957). I heard that it was commissioned at the recommendation of Kuniharu Akiyama. And this piece is dedicated to Fumio Hayasaka.

T: Yes, it was premiered by the Tōkyō Symphony Orchestra conducted by Hitoshi Ueda. Mr. Akiyama was the editor-in-chief of the bulletin of that organization and recommended Tōru for the commission. He started to write *Requiem for Strings*, but meanwhile, Mr. Hayasaka passed away from tuberculosis. So Tōru decided to dedicate the *Requiem* to Mr. Hayasaka. Tōru also realized that he might not live long himself, because of his own ill health at that time.

O: According to the records, the premiere performance was on June 20th, 1957 at Hibiya Kōkaidō Hall. Were you at the premiere?

T: Yes, I remember going to Hibiya Kōkaidō Hall from Kamakura. But the review wasn't that good. The critic from Yomiuri Newspaper wrote, "It needs more structure."

O: In reference to *Lento in Due Movimenti*, Ginji Yamane expressed his sentiment in writing that "it is pre-music," but he gave more favorable review regarding *Requiem for Strings*. Was there a big audience in the concert hall?

T: I think there were a lot of people.

O: In time, this piece received the highest praise from Stravinsky. When Stravinsky arrived in Japan in 1959, did Takemitsu meet him?

T: Yes, we were invited to a party at a hotel in Shinagawa or one in Takanawa, Tōkyō. Later, Stravinsky wrote, "that music as intense as this should be created by a man of such short stature…"[32] Then Tōru said, "Funny he says that. He himself is also so short! Then people can say the *Rite of Spring* was created by a man of such short stature…" [*laughs*] Tōru shook hands with Stravinsky at the party and recalled that his hand was very soft and big.

O: That is so funny. [*laughs*] Stravinsky's "a man of short stature…" is now a famous quote, but do you know when Stravinsky listened to his music?

T: Hmm, I wonder. While visiting NHK broadcast station, Stravinsky listened to some works by Japanese composers, and maybe it was one of them.

O: That is probably right. Our editorial team also researched this, and it is highly probable that Stravinsky listened to the recording of the NHK Symphony's 1958 performance conducted by Masashi Mori.

T: That could be right. Then it attracted Stravinsky's attention. The other day, film director Masahiro Shinoda asked to use *Requiem for Strings* in his movie *Spy Sorge* (2003), for the scene where young soldiers are executed in the *2.26 Jiken* ('February 26 incident').[33] The main score was done by Shinichirō Ikebe, so the *Requiem* was only for that scene. I watched the pre-screening with my daughter Maki, and she said, "This piece is

---

[32] The original phrase was reported in Donald Richie, 'Tokyo no Stravinsky', *Ongaku Geijutsu*, Sept. 1959.
[33] *2.26 Jiken*: the attempted coup d'état by the young officers of the Japanese Imperial Army that took place Feb. 26-29, 1936.

actually pretty good. The rest of daddy's pieces sound the same." [*laughs*] That means his next forty years were in vain. [*laughs*]

O: By the way, do you know whether *Scene* for cello and string orchestra (1955) was written around the same time as *Requiem*?

T: I don't think he wrote it in Kamakura, perhaps it was when we were still in Senzoku-Ike. I thought it was before *Requiem*? But I don't remember much about it. Maybe it was written in parallel with *Requiem*. The conductor Hiroyuki Iwaki[34] didn't remember either, so maybe it was in Kamakura. Tōru never said much about *Scene, Chamber Concerto*, and *Landscape* (1960), so he probably thought they were not well written.

O: In the *Complete Takemitsu Edition*, we asked Hiroyuki Iwaki and Ensemble Kanazawa to record this piece, and Takemitsu's friend and composer Teizō Matsumura was there at the studio. He said, "I can recognize Takemitsu's music even looking at it upside down."

T: That's interesting. I heard that the score is picturesque and graphic like. Even looking at the score upside down, you can see Tōru's uniqueness.

Shūzō Takiguchi

O: When Takemitsu was hospitalized in Keiō Hospital, he had received many letters from Shūzō Takiguchi.[35] How was his relationship with Mr. Takiguchi?

T: I think his encounter with Mr. Takiguchi made a big impact on Tōru's life. Tōru was interested not only in music, but also in art, including surrealism—and this was when not many Japanese were interested in, nor had knowledge of, surrealism. Kuniharu Akiyama taught him a lot about surrealism. And they obtained several pre-war volumes of the

---

[34] Hiroyuki Iwaki (1932-2006): Japanese conductor who advocated contemporary works. He premiered many Takemitsu's works; *Solitude Sonore* (1958), *Textures* (1964).
[35] Shūzō Takiguchi (1903-79): poet, art critic. He introduced surrealism and avant-garde art to Japan. He was a mentor to Takemitsu and the members of *Jikken Kōbō*.

journal *Shi to Shiron* ('Poetry and Poetics') and found that Mr. Takiguchi wrote about surrealism. Then Tōru became interested in it, and started visiting Mr. Takiguchi. He respected Mr. Takiguchi for his way of life as well as his views on art and poetry. Mr. Takiguchi went through hard times during the war—being arrested as a political offender and losing his house during the bombing of Tōkyō—but he continued to study during those hard times and lived a humble life throughout. He continued to host a series at the Takemiya Gallery that introduced unknown young artists. Many young artists were recognized and became popular after presenting their works there.

O: Mr. Takiguchi also was fond of Tōru.

T: Yes, Mr. Takiguchi was not directly involved in music, but he was very nice to Tōru and half-jokingly asked him to become his adopted son. Tōru always visited him when the opportunity arose and never forgot to visit him at the end of the year.[36] He was very happy to see Mr. Takiguchi and would talk with him at least once a month. So you can say that Tōru's mentor and teacher in a real sense was Mr. Takiguchi. There was one incident—this was before we started living together and Tōru couldn't even pay the rental fee for his Erard piano—when Mr. Takiguchi visited Tōru's room and after he left, Tōru cleaned up the floor cushion and found money under it. And this was when Mr. Takiguchi didn't even have money either. After Mr. Takiguchi moved to Ochiai near Shinjuku, Tōru was given money unexpectedly whenever he visited. He helped Tōru in so many ways. Since Tōru always looked so shabby, Mr. Takiguchi gave him his own gray-colored half coat. Tōru wore that gray coat for many years to come.

O: There is a photo of Tōru and Yasuji Kiyose at the *Shin-Sakkyokuha Kyōkai* ('Association of New School of Composition') with many others. Was that the gray coat from Takiguchi?

T: Yes, that is the one. [*laughs*] Tōru was really poor at that time. He didn't have a stable income for a long time, and it was only during the last ten years that we didn't have to worry about money. I always said, "Next month is alright, but we won't have money in two or three

---

36 Around New Years' day, people would visit their seniors bearing small gifts as a means of thanks.

months." [*laughs*] But if we had two or three months worth of money, I was relieved. When we lived in Kamakura, Yoshio Mamiya[37] and other people came to visit us and often said, "I wish we could have six months worth of money." Several decades later, we met and said, "Well, our situation hasn't changed that much. What should we do next year?" [*laughs*]

---

[37] Yoshio Mamiya (1929-): Japanese composer. He collected and arranged *minyō* (Japanese folk music), and wrote the music for the anime *Grave of the Fireflies* (1988).

Chapter 2

Movie Fanatic

In this part of the interview, Asaka reveals Takemitsu's father (who died young) and his mother, who was a free-spirited and independent woman for her time, and who raised Tōru as a single mother. Later, Asaka addresses her own life with their daughter, Maki. Although rambling, a central thread emerges in the Takemitsu clan's love for movies. As her comments suggest, film music may have played a more important role in Takemitsu's development as a composer than has been previously thought.

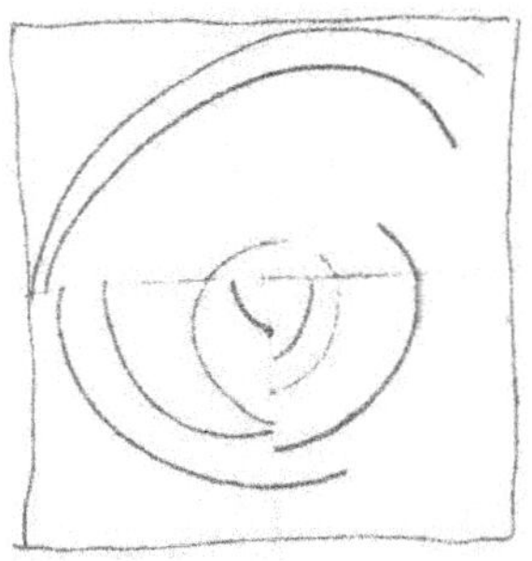

I want to go to school in Japan

O'hara: Takemitsu was born in Tōkyō, but I heard that soon after his birth his family moved to Dalian[1] in China. Then at the age of seven, he returned to Japan without his parents.

Takemitsu: Yes, I wonder why he thought of such a thing. He told his parents that he wanted to go to elementary school in Japan. So they took him to the airport, and he flew back to Japan all alone. The plane was probably related to the military. In Japan, he was cared for by his uncle in Hongō, Tōkyō. I can't believe he returned to Japan by himself while his parents were still in Manchuria! His aunt was a *koto*[2] master of the Ikuta School. Since they lost their two sons in the war, his aunt's *koto* playing was always somber and lonely, and Tōru often overheard the couple arguing. So Tōru had bitter memories of the *koto*.

O: His parents eventually returned to Japan from Dalian, didn't they?

T: Tōru's father, mother and his two younger sisters returned to Japan, but his father became ill and moved back to his hometown of Kagoshima in Kyūshū. Shortly thereafter, Tōru's father passed away. There is an interesting story behind his father's death. Tōru was looking out his classroom window in Tōkyō when, suddenly, he 'saw' his father in a coat standing in the schoolyard. Tōru remembered his relatives wondering, "This boy doesn't shed any tears upon hearing the sad news of his father's passing." After his father's passing, his mother and his younger sisters moved from Kagoshima to Tōkyō, and the three of them started to live in Komagome, Tōkyō.[3] His mother returned to her old job with the Yasuda Fire Insurance Company, but Tōru remained at his uncle's house so that he didn't have to transfer schools. At his uncle's house, he used to go to Hongō Cinema Theater with his cousins, and he started seeing movies around that time. But the effects of the war on certain areas were severe, so his two sisters

---

[1] Dalian: city in the south of the Liáodōng Peninsula in China. Under the Russian occupation, Dalian became a base for trade. Coming under Japanese rule in 1905, it continued to develop as an industrial center.

[2] *Koto:* a traditional Japanese string instrument. There are two distinct schools of *koto* playing, Ikuta and Yamada; the former uses a square pick and latter a round pick.

[3] Komagome: belongs to Toshima ward, located in northwest Tōkyō.

moved to the countryside as student evacuees. Since his mother was all alone, Tōru left his uncle's house and started living with his mother.

O: So after coming back to Japan and entering elementary school, mother and son were finally able to live together.

T: That's right. When he lived in Komagome, Tōru was good at making fires in their *shichirin*.[4] He used old papers from his mother's office to start the fire, then would cook rice in the *shichirin* while waiting for his mother to come home. His mother used to say that Tōru's rice was very delicious. I heard this story from Tōru's sister. Probably his mother was sharing memories of the past and told this story to her daughter later on.

O: I heard Komagome suffered from a very bad air raid.

T: Yes. Their house in Komagome was burned down, and when Tōru was fifteen years old, his uncle's house in Hongō was also destroyed during the Great Tōkyō Air Raid in March 1945. So after the war, Tōru, his two sisters, and his mother started to live in Setagaya-Daita.

O: I see. That is when you became neighbors.

T: That is right.

Tōru's mother loved movies

O: I recall that Takemitsu's mother really loved movies. Do you think Tōru inherited his love for movies from his mother?

T: I think there is some connection there. She liked movies all her life, and in her later years she would even sit in the aisle if the theater was full. In her youth, she studied English very hard out of sheer desire to write letters to Hollywood. There were many movie-related books in her house. I heard that when she read a book that she thought was

---

[4] *Shichirin*: a portable clay stove that uses charcoal.

suitable for a movie, she would send a plot summary to the president of Daiei Motion Picture Company.[5] [*laughs*] There is another funny story. Once, when my mother-in-law was strolling near Takarazuka Theater in the Yūrakuchō district, she met the famous actress Kyōko Anzai[6] on the street. Anzai was so beautiful that Tōru's mother said to her, "I thought you were beautiful on the screen, but you look even more beautiful in person." Anzai responded simply, "Thank you very much." [*laughs*] Anyway, she loved movies.

O: Wow. She really was a fanatic! [*laughs*]

T: As a New Year's tradition after our marriage, we used to visit my mother-in-law's house, then pray at a temple in Asakusa, and then go see movies together. I didn't like traditional period dramas, such as the *Hatamoto Taikutsu-Otoko*[7] films with Utaemon Ichikawa, but I learned a lot about James Dean and Elvis Presley from her. In her later years, she became a fan of Yūjirō Ishihara[8] and she took the Chinese character from Yū-jirō and named her granddaughter (Tōru's niece) 'Yū-ko.' My mother-in-law also taught me how to play *mahjong*.[9]

O: Were there any other similarities between Takemitsu and his mother?

T: Yes. She seemed relaxed and carefree in general, but there was a side of her that could be strangely obsessive. If we arranged to meet each other at a certain place, she would come at least ten minutes early. Even when I was punctual, she would say, "You're late!" Tōru was also like that. When we planned to go out and I was a little late getting myself ready, he would say, "I'm gonna go first" and leave the house

---

[5] Daiei Motion Picture: founded in 1942, it was one of the major motion picture companies at that time. Kurosawa's *Rashōmon* was produced by Daiei.

[6] Kyōko Anzai (1934-2002): Japanese actress popular in the 1950s.

[7] *Hatamoto Taikutsu-otoko* was a popular period drama set in Edo period Japan (1603-1868). Utaemon Ichikawa took the lead role as the Shōgun Tokugawa throughout the entire series of thirty-one films.

[8] Yūjiro Ishihara (1934-87): Japanese actor and singer. His talent as the singer came to the fore in the film *Crazed Fruit,* for which Takemitsu and Masaru Satō composed music. After that, he was active both as an actor and a popular song singer.

[9] *Mahjong* began in China and spread to Japan in 1910. After World War II, it was still played in many households.

without me. At that time, the Seibu Line ran every twenty minutes and we always discussed which train to take. So sometimes, he would arrive at the station early enough to catch the previous train. Even when he arrived early enough to buy me a train ticket, he wouldn't. [*laughs*] My mother-in-law's handbag was well-organized inside. She put different types of stamps in separate plastic bags. Tōru had a similar side.

O: It sounds like his meticulous nature was also inherited from his mother. Did Takemitsu regularly meet deadlines for his compositions?

T: Even in his younger days, his desktop was very well-organized, and I think he met his deadlines pretty well. He used to say that in order to get a good performance for his work, the musicians needed to see their parts early. But film music and theater music were different. He saw a rush one day and had to compose music for it by the next day in order to meet the deadline.

O: Did Takemitsu's mother see any of the movies that Tōru scored?

T: I think she saw his movies. But she never came to a live concert. She didn't want to get involved in things that she was not interested in…Tōru actually appreciated that kind of attitude from his mother. Usually, a widowed mother tends to put too much pressure on her son, but Tōru's mother didn't oppose him when he said he wanted to be a composer. She was a very independent woman for her generation.

O: She was a pioneering career-driven woman.

T: Yes, she was a forerunner. She was able to work and support herself. She used to say, "I was the first one in Japan to have my hair permed." It won't seem strange to us nowadays, but she dyed part of her hair purple! Anyway, she had a strong personality, and if she believed something was good, she didn't care what other people thought. Even her clothes were unique. I hope I can be like that. [*laughs*]

Tōru and mother in Dalian, China.

O: For example, what kind of clothes?

T: Since she worked in an office, she wore Western-style clothes during the summer, but Japanese-style dress during the winter. She used to say, "I am ahead of Sueko Ōtsuka."[10] She sewed *kimono* by herself using wool fabric, and tied the *obi* (the kimono belt) in a butterfly knot rather than the typical square shape.

O: I bet she attracted a lot of attention.

T: You bet she did! [*laughs*] My daughter Maki used to say, "I don't want to walk with her. It's embarrassing." But these are all fond memories now. She was also good at knitting, and would knit things for me and Maki along with her own clothes. She knew a person in the foreign merchant section of the Matsuya Department Store in Ginza and, when she went to the store, she would copy out the designs of the latest trends and would knit a top and bottom outfit.

O: Didn't Tōru say anything about her outlandish outfits?

T: Well, he said he didn't like it, but there was nothing that he could do. [*laughs*]

O: The mother and son didn't meddle with each other. [*laughs*]

T: There are some peculiar people from that generation you know.

O: Yes, there are many interesting people who lived in the Taishō era.[11]

T: Many carried on in their own way, especially in the arts. On top of it, Tōru's mother lived outside Japan for a while. There are many unique individuals who grew up on the continent (Manchuria, China), such as

---

10 Sueko Ōtsuka: dress designer who incorporated modern, Western techniques into traditional Japanese designs. She is sometimes credited with inventing the 'modern' *kimono*.

11 The Taishō period (1912-1926): a time when the latest in European and American culture and modern flowed into Japan and a modern lifestyle arose. Men began to dress in Western clothes and many Western-style buildings—department stores, cafés and dance halls—were constructed.

Seiji Ozawa[12] and Kōbō Abe.[13] Tōru was raised by parents who absorbed the spirit of freedom, so maybe he was likewise relatively more unique than others.

O: Do you know anything about Takemitsu's father?

T: Tōru's father died when he was seven years old, so I only heard about him through Tōru and his mother. Tōru's parents met at the insurance company—the Yasuda Fire Insurance Company—where his mother worked as a typist. When Tōru was born, she quit the company and then her husband was transferred to Dalian in Manchuria.

O: It was before the war—a time of relative freedom on the continent.

T: I heard that Tōru's parents enjoyed social dancing in Manchuria. His father would brew beer illegally and hide it underground. As he didn't like to go to work in the morning, his mother had to push him out the door. Before moving to Manchuria, he worked as an umpire at Jingū Stadium for the Tōkyō Big Six University baseball league.[14] He was also a master of birdcalls. When he whistled through his fingers, many birds would fly to him.

O: So he had many hobbies! Master of bird calling—maybe he had a good ear for music.

T: On top of it, he played *shakuhachi*.[15] Tōru stayed in Manchuria until he was six years old, but his father liked Dixieland jazz very much, and he remembered listening to recordings on his father's phonograph. Before the war, social dance was very popular, and Tōru remembered

[12] Seiji Ozawa (1935-): Japanese conductor, born in present day Shenyang, China. He conducted the premieres of several of Takemitsu's works, including *November Steps* (1967), *Quatrain* (1975), *Dream/Window* (1985), and *Ceremonial* (1992).
[13] Kōbō Abe (1924- 1993): Japanese writer and playwright. Born in Tōkyō, he lived in present day Shenyang City, China between the age of one and twenty-two. His works are known for their absurd worlds and surrealistic atmosphere.
[14] Tōkyō Big Six: an intercollegiate baseball league, consisting of teams from six universities in the Tokyo area: Hōsei University, Keiō University, Meiji University, Rikkyō University, University of Tōkyō, Waseda University.
[15] *Shakuhachi*: traditional Japanese end-blown flute made of bamboo. Takemitsu used *shakuhachi* in his famous work, *November Steps* (1967).

that whenever his parents had a dance contest the next day, they would practice the steps while looking at instruction sheets. They entered several contests in Dalian and won one of them.

O: Amazing. Do you dance, too?

T: Oh, no no. [*laughs*]

O: Within Japan, militarism created a tense atmosphere, but it was rather more liberal overseas.

T: I think some overseas residents had a good life and were able to breathe a more liberal air. I once saw a photo of Tōru's family in Dalian with a big German Sheppard, but my family was forced to give up our dog to the government. You can see how different it was from domestic Japan. When I look back, their lifestyle came at the cost of the Manchurian people though. Tōru's family was lucky enough to return to Japan before the end of the war, but people who came back after the war struggled greatly. Around the time that Tōru returned to Japan, the whole country was heading toward militarism. The first thing we did when we went to school in the morning was to salute in the direction of the Emperor's residence. When I look back at the war years in Japan, I simply cannot laugh at North Korea now. While militarism was getting stronger domestically, Tōru's parents were able to live freely and openly in Dalian. I think his mother's personality was cultivated in that kind of environment.

O: I imagine you and Takemitsu's mother got along pretty well.

T: We were different people, but I think we did get along well. Even when Tōru was not home, his mother would come over and say, "As long as Asaka-san and Maki-chan are here, I want to come over." She always listened to what I had to say. So I didn't experience any of the typical wife and mother-in-law conflicts.

O: Did you and Tōru quarrel sometimes?

T: We didn't have any serious fights, but we often argued over small things. But he used to say he could not compose when we were in discord, so he would tell me, "I'm sorry" even if he didn't mean it, and then ran off. He used to say, "If I had enough money for compensation, I could divorce you anytime." He was joking but I took it seriously and became depressed. Then he would forget all about it and come to talk to me again. [*laughs*] When Maki was a schoolgirl, they had a huge fight which developed into a scuffle. Tōru broke the doorknob, and I was so worried that I hid the knives in the kitchen. Feeling upset, I locked myself in my room, but they had already reconciled and called out to me, "Hey, why don't you come over here. There's a funny program on TV." They were giggling together watching TV. Then he said to Maki, "Your mother shouldn't go on living in the past. She is bad." [*laughs*]

The Whole Family Loved Movies!

O: Your daughter Maki became a movie subtitle translator.

T: Maki preferred sports when she was younger, but Tōru told her, "You don't have to study, but see more movies." In high school, Maki went to Boston as an exchange student, and her host family often took her to see movies on weekends, saying that it was a good way to learn English. So one thing led to another, and before she knew it, she loved movies. Her first job as a subtitle translator was for *Promised Land*,[16] and Tōru and I went to the theater to see it. We were such doting parents. When we saw 'Translator: Maki Takemitsu' on the screen, we cheered loudly, "Yeah!" [*laughs*] But that was it. After that, Tōru wasn't interested in knowing what kind of work she was doing.

O: You like movies as much as Tōru, don't you?

---

[16] *Promised Land* (1987): an American movie directed by Michael Hoffman. It came to Japan in 1989.

Takemitsu and daughter Maki

T: Yes, ever since childhood. Even before the war, my sister, who was ten years older, brought me to see French movies. We went to several movie theaters in the Shinjuku area such as Kōonza, Teitoza, and Musashino-kan. So once I met Tōru, we both bragged about which movies we already knew. Tōru saw all kinds of films including period dramas, *chambara* (swordfight movies), and ghost stories. But I saw more foreign movies, so I was proud and talked a lot about it. During the war, English movies were prohibited, but we were able to see German and French films—for instance the French-made *Prison sans Barreax* and German-made *Hometown*—in Ikebukuro on the way back from the 'school factory.'

O: 'School factory'? Was that for labor mobilization?

T: We called it 'school factory.' I went to a Catholic girl's school, but they were prohibited from holding church services during the war and the chapel became a storage room for military hardware. Then the school turned into a factory. We worked there, but went to the theater secretly on the way home from school. If somebody had discovered us, we would've been in big trouble. Seeing movies was considered somewhat delinquent. But there were no other entertainments, like today. We just had movies.

O: Wow, you had courage to do that…I imagine there weren't many people who went to see movies during the war.

T: Actually, many people saw them secretly. My sister's husband liked movies and he worked for customs in Yokohama. After the war started, American films were seized by the Yokohama customs office. One of those films was *Gone with the Wind*, so he saw it secretly at his work. At my girls' school, we secretly passed around books such as *Gone with the Wind* and *Rebecca*. Even those kinds of books were censored.

O: It sounds like movies were the link between you and Takemitsu.

T: That may be right. With Tōru, movies were the best things to share.

O: Did you go see many movies after you got married?

T: Yes. Even when we were first dating, we used to talk about movies and go see them together. When a film magazine invited us to write an essay on *Children of Paradise* ('Les Enfants du Paradis'), Tōru said to me, "It's boring to write a normal review, so let's do it together and write it like a debate." I wrote my part in earnest by the deadline, but Tōru didn't draft anything! [*laughs*] When we started talking about movies, we couldn't stop for hours, even in later years. Many composers dedicate their own pieces to their wives or lovers, right? Tōru always dedicated his pieces to his daughter or friends, but never to me. But his collection of essays about movies, *Quotation of Dream* ('Yume no Inyō'),[17]—*that* he dedicated to me. He wrote: "To my wife who is my eternal movie companion, with deepest appreciation." [*laughs*]

O: Do you remember which movies you went to see together when you were young?

---

[17] *Quotation of Dream*, Iwanami Shoten, 1984. In 1991, Takemitsu composed a work for two pianos and orchestra also entitled *Quotation of Dream*.

T: *Manon* and Laurence Olivier's *Wuthering Heights* were very striking. One of Tōru's relatives worked at Shōchiku Movie Company, so he invited us to see the pre-screening. We were both excited to see *West Side Story*. I remember talking to Tōru about *A Star is Born* to Tōru. When the leading role girl is about to leave her home, and dreams of being a star, she confides only in her grandmother. One scene, the grandmother sitting on rocking chair knitting, made a strong impression on me as a child. But watching forty years later, this time on laser disc, I found that the grandmother sitting on a rocking chair and her knitting were two separate scenes. I said to Tōru, "Movie memories are interesting." Later, Tōru stole my idea and wrote an essay about movie memories. Not fair! [*laughs*]

O: That's a copyright violation. [*laughs*]

T: He was often cheeky like that. There was a movie called *The Farmer's Daughter* starring Loretta Young that came out right after the war, and I was startled by the numerous cultural differences between Japan and the U.S. The girl used a brush not a comb, and there was a large closet in her bedroom and so many dresses hung in it. In Japan, there were only small dressers, so while a coat could fit, other clothes were usually kept in the drawers. When Tōru went to the University of Louisville in Minnesota to receive the Louisville Grawemeyer Award for Music and Composition,[18] he gave a speech at the ceremony saying, "I saw this movie called *The Farmer's Daughter* after the war..." as if he actually saw the movie. Of course the people in Minnesota loved it. [*laughs*]

O: He probably felt as if he saw it himself because your description was so vivid.

T: In his later years, when I saw a movie first he would ask me, "What? When did you see it? How was it?" And then later, he would talk to Maki as if he actually saw it himself. [*laughs*] We competed to see movies that we couldn't go together. The first one to see it wins! All three of us were competing.

---

[18] Louisville Grawemeyer Award for Music and Composition: an international musical award begun in 1984 by the H. Charles Grawemeyer Foundation. Takemitsu won the award in 1994 for his *Fantasma/ Cantos* for clarinet and orchestra.

O: I heard that Takemitsu saw about three hundred films. Did you see that many, too?

T: I saw about as many as he did, but only for a brief period of time. In Kamakura, even if we didn't have money for next month's rent, we would go pawn something at the shop and then see a movie. Does Shiminza Theater still exist in Kamakura?

O: No, Kamakura has lost all its movie theaters. Theatre Kamakura was the last one.

T: There used to be the Theatre Kamakura behind the station, Shiminza near the town hall, Tōei on Komachi street, Daiei straight down on Ura street, and a theater for foreign movies near Rokujizō.

O: How many theaters were there back then?

T: There were five. We always went whenever the movies changed.

O: But in Kamakura, I imagine that your life was already tough financially with Takemitsu's limited income from composing, so I wonder if you had to sacrifice food expenses in order to see movies so often. [*laughs*]

T: [*Big laugh*] Well, at that time, food and clothing were very simple. We had one formal outfit and wore it every time we went out. It was like that all over Japan, so we didn't feel particularly miserable. We tried to manage things so that we could go to the movies. Nowadays I can catch a taxi on the way home, but at that time we always walked home. There were no houses on the way back, so it was very dark and frightening. One time, I saw Akira Kurosawa's *Throne of Blood* ('Kumonosu-jō') at Theatre Kamakura. The movie was scary, and on the way home the street was dark and I went through an empty tunnel. It was so, so scary…

O: Maybe a thief from the *Throne of Blood* was hiding out?…[*laughs*]

T: Oh, I remember my heart pounding all the way home.

When Takemitsu started film music

O: I heard that Takemitsu first began to compose music for film as an assistant to Fumio Hayasaka. Was that before you got married?

T: Yes, he needed to support himself, so he went to Mr. Hayasaka's house to help him orchestrate the full score and to copy out parts. He first assisted with the score to *Rashōmon*.[19] Later Tōru said that it was a very good practical learning experience for him. Young composers have few opportunities to have their music performed, especially if they write an orchestral work. But film scores get turned into sound almost immediately. He wasn't the one who was composing the actual music, but by helping to write out the score and parts, he was able to see that, "If the notes are layered this way" then, "Aha, it will sound like this when it is performed." Tōru said that since he didn't attend any formal music school, his true study of music began with Mr. Hayasaka. With Yasuji Kiyose,[20] he just brought over some study pieces and received a bit of feedback and heard a few lectures on music.

O: I heard that Takemitsu was knowledgeable about scripts too.

T: Yes. When Tōru first met the film director Masahiro Shinoda[21] at the Ōfuna film studio, he told him that he had already read the script to Shinoda's *One Way Ticket to Love* (1960) in a magazine. Mr. Shinoda was very happy to hear that.

---

[19] *Rashōmon* (1950): Japanese movie directed by Akira Kurosawa. It won a Venice Film Festival Golden Lion award and an Academy Award in the United States. It was the first Japanese movie to receive critical international acclaim.

[20] Yasuji Kiyose (1900-81): Japanese composer. Kiyose sought to incorporate elements of traditional Japanese music, such as pentatonic scales and Japanese folk song, into his own compositions. Takemitsu was impressed by his *Violin Sonata*, and he asked to become his pupil in 1948.

[21] Masahiro Shinoda (1931-): movie director. He joined Shōchiku in 1953 and established his own film company Hyōgensha in 1966. Takemitsu composed music scores for sixteen of Shinoda's movies.

O: When Shinoda went to Kamakura to commission Takemitsu for *Dried Lake* ('Kawaita Mizuumi'), you were both fighting tuberculosis. Do you remember anything about that?

T: Yes, I do. Mr. Shinoda came to see us at our house when we were sick in bed.

O: When you lived in Kamakura, Takemitsu composed film music for the Shōchiku Company.[22]

T: Tōru began working at the Ōfuna film studio to help Toshirō Mayuzumi complete a score commission. Mayuzumi had asked Tōru in a considerate way, "I have an emergency and cannot do this film, so please take this work." Mayuzumi had already notified the company staff about it before Tōru spoke with them. Since we lived close to the film studio, Tōru started to compose film scores for the director Noboru Nakamura too.[23] I have a strong impression of *Dewdrops* ('Tsuyu no Atosaki,'1956) and *Pouring Rain* ('Doshaburi,'1957), but Tōru wasn't fond of the Shōchiku-Ōfuna type melodramas. His last work for Shōchiku was *The Kii River* ('Kino-kawa,'1966). In one scene, the bride gets married on a boat in the Kii River and Tōru composed funeral-like music. The company's executives got mad and they had a huge fight over it. They said they could never work with a composer who lacks such common sense as to use funeral music in a wedding ceremony. [*laughs*]

O: But he won a Mainichi Film Award in the music category for *The Kii River* in 1966. [*laughs*]

T: Yes, that's right. [*laughs*] Speaking of Shōchiku, Tōru was involved in a car accident once on the way back from the Shōchiku film studio. In the middle of the night, a train and his taxi collided on the sidetrack

---

[22] Shōchiku Company: Japanese major film company established in 1902. Directors, Nagisa Ōshima, Masahiro Shinoda and Yoshishige Yoshida also belonged to this company but left in the1960's.

[23] Noboru Nakamura (1938-81): movie director. He joined Shōchiku in 1936. Takemitsu composed music for twelve films, including *Red and Green* ('Shu to Midori' (1956), *Twin Sisters of Kyōtō* (1963), and *The Kii River* (1966).

used by cargo trains, and the taxi fell into a rice field nearby. Tōru stayed at home for a while. After the accident, the taxi driver—looking very worried— came to visit with a big fruit basket and said, "I had to stop working, and may lose my job." So we felt bad for him and Tōru said, "It's OK. I am fine." [*laughs*] But actually after the accident, he had headaches and didn't feel well, so he couldn't work for a while. Everyone scolded him and said that he needed to ask the taxi company for compensation.

O: I heard that many friends came to visit your house in Kamakura.

T: Yes, Tōru later said that Kamakura was the happiest time in his life. He was sick but still young and had more stamina. His friends were not too busy at that time so that they could visit often and stay over. Tōru spent most of the time in Kamakura recuperating, but when he was feeling better, he and his friends would go to the beach, or compete in quick shot using a toy pistol (as in Westerns) or play poker. Shuntarō Tanikawa was already driving a car, which was quite rare at that time.

O: It seems that Takemitsu crossed with so many people during that time.

T: Yes, writers such as Hiroshi Sakagami[24] and Katao Yamakawa, and Mr. Sakagami's friend Michiharu Mochizuki came to visit us often. They did all sorts of things together. They went to the shooting gallery in Enoshima, and imitated the Nichigeki dance team line dancers. Mr. Yamakawa was good at mimicking actor's poses in Sharaku's woodblock prints.[25] He copied these so well that we would all burst out laughing. Mr. Sakagami was only nineteen but he had already left his parent's house to live with an elder lady and was writing novels. His novel *My Son, His Lover* ('Musuko to Koibito') became a candidate for the Akutagawa Prize.[26] Tōru was very impressed. He was very delighted

---

24 Hiroshi Sakagami (1936-): Japanese novelist. While student at Keio University, he published *My Son, His Lover* in the magazine Mita Bungaku.
25 Tōshūsai Sharaku: One of the great masters of woodblock printing in the Edo era (ca. 1800).
26 Akutagawa Prize: named after Ryūnosuke Akutagawa, the foremost writer in the Taishō period. This is Japan's most sought after literary prize.

to spend time with people younger than he was. Keita Asari[27] was only twenty when he started Shiki Theatre Company, so everyone was young. Mr. Asari also visited us in Kamakura. When we lived in Senzoku-Ike, the Shiki Theatre's practice studio was nearby, so Tōru used to hang out with Takeshi Kusaka and Hiroshi Mizushima and other actors. They liked to play word games, writing 'when' 'where' 'who' 'did what' randomly on separate pieces of paper, and then assembling them into a story. They would also invent vulgar words. [*laughs*] Tōru's musician friends were more refined and didn't engage in such trivial pranks, so this was a breath of fresh air for Tōru and he had great fun. But through those silly pranks, he made connections with various people.

O: Over the years, didn't Takemitsu's circle of friends extend across many different fields of art?

T: Yes, when I look back on it now, and I really think he was so blessed to meet all these people.

O: On an interview tape in NHK an anchorman once asked him, "How did you become a composer?" He answered, "If you keep on thinking, your wish will come true."

T: Yes, he had an optimistic side to him. Once he became a composer, he didn't worry too much about being able to make it as a musician. He just composed because he wanted to. Maybe he made it because he kept on thinking, but probably luck played a big part in it too. I think he had a lot of luck.

O: Maybe the encounter with Asaka-san was the best luck for Takemitsu...

T: I wonder about that...As I said it before, Mr. Akiyama said that Tōru became more boring after meeting Mr. Tanikawa and me. He did become less ruthless and less exciting, but I let him do what he wanted

---

[27] Keita Asari (1933-): Japanese stage director. He founded Shiki Theatre Company in 1953 while still a student at Keiō University. Takemitsu collaborated with Asari in twelve theater works.

to do. He had a life-threatening disease so I may have been carping too much, but I did what I had to do. [*laughs*]

O: Perhaps he possessed some sort of aura that led other people to feel that they had to help him out…

T: Or maybe it was just pure luck…When he started out as a composer, he met many friends in *Jikken Kōbō*; he met Yasushi Akutagawa; he received a piano from Mr. Mayuzumi. He was helped by so many people.

O: Composing is a lonely process, but making music is done by many people.

T: Yes. Composing is a tough job, but music making cannot be done alone. There are people who perform it and people who listen to it. And there are people who provide performance opportunities. Tōru met more and more people through this process, and he was given the joy of composing through meeting these wonderful people. I think he was so lucky to have such an opportunity. After the war, Tōru's generation started from scratch. They were poor but in a way, they were lucky and blessed.

New Experiment

O: In the 1960's, Takemitsu started collaborating with film directors of his generation, such as Masahiro Shinoda and Hiroshi Teshigahara. They broke with the major film companies and started working independently.[28] Takemitsu produced many new film scores at a time when he was also composing for concert music.

T: Yes, that's right.

---

[28] Hiroshi Teshigahara (1927-2001): Japanese movie director. Takemitsu composed the music for *The Pitfall* (1962), *Woman in the Dunes* (1964), *Face of Another* (1966), and *Rikyū* (1989).

O: Takemitsu used *biwa*[29] and *shakuhachi* in Shinoda's *The Assassin* ('Ansatsu,' 1964), and in *Kwaidan* (1965) by Masaki Kobayashi.[30] Shortly thereafter he also began to use traditional Japanese instruments in *November Steps* (1967) and other concert works. It seems like this was a major step for him, but was there a particular reason for it at the time?

T: Well…[*long silence*] He used *shakuhachi* in *The Assassin* and *biwa* in *Kwaidan*, but it wasn't like he was suddenly inspired by Japanese instruments or had some eye-opening experience. I think the younger people can readily accept the sound of traditional Japanese instruments as they are, but for Tōru's generation, we could not think of these sounds without envisioning the feudalistic ideals and apprentice systems associated with them. Due to the war experience, our generation avoided things Japanese for a certain period of time on purpose. But after a while, once Tōru liberated himself from his preconceptions and actually listened to performances with traditional Japanese instruments, the sounds began to possess a certain power and fascination. He was rather surprised to find such instruments in Japan. Before using Japanese traditional instruments in his concert music, he used to say it was strange to use Western instruments in Japanese period dramas without even thinking about it. It would sound more natural to use traditional instruments in period dramas. Then around that time, he was asked to compose the score for *Kwaidan*. In the film's third story—*Hōichi the Earless*—the main character plays the *biwa*, and so Tōru started to learn about it. After he used *biwa* and *shakuhachi* in these period dramas, he said jokingly, "It's so funny that everybody is surprised."

O: How did he meet Kinshi Tsuruta,[31] the famous *biwa* player?

---

[29] *Biwa*: traditional Japanese instrument of the lute family. There are six different types of biwa/styles of playing. Takemitsu composed for the Satsuma biwa.

[30] Masaki Kobayashi (1916-96): Japanese movie director. Takemitsu composed music for all of Kobayashi's films since 1962: *Harakiri* (1962), *Kwaidan* (1964), *Tōkyō Trial* (1983) and others.

[31] Kinshi Tsuruta (1911-95): Satsuma *biwa* player and composer. She, along with *shakuhachi* player Katsuya Yokoyama, helped to premiere Takemitsu's *Eclipse* and *November Steps*.

T: The writer Kunio Tsuji's father was a *biwa* player and Tōru studied *biwa* with him. He wanted to do something new in the war scene of the movie *Kwaidan*, and he asked whether Tsuji knew a *biwa* player who could perform on the sound track. Tsuji said, "Before the war there was a genius female *biwa* player, but I haven't heard what has happened to her since. She is a real genius and can do innovative things." Then Tōru looked her up and went to visit her. She lived in a huge mansion and a lady came to the door and said, "She is out playing *pachinko*[32] now."

O: Was she the maid?

T: No, no. Ms. Tsuruta was living with that lady. She was very pretty and went to look for Ms. Tsuruta, and then came back with a person wearing a suit. Tōru was so surprised because he thought Ms. Tsuruta was a 'female' *biwa* player. But when he talked to this person, she had a female voice and said, "I don't play *biwa* now, but I will do it if it's that much fun."

O: She hadn't played *biwa* for a long time, then?

T: After the war, she was a successful businesswoman, but back then there were many obstacles for women working in business, so she started to dress like a man. There was a period before the war when *biwa* was popular, but there was some kind of a scandal and she was forced to quit performing *biwa*. She had a talent for business, and earned lots of money by managing real estate, cabarets, and pubs. She said, "In those days, women were looked down upon, so I became a man." [*laughs*]

O: So she had a talent in business. She was a woman acting as a man.

T: After I became close to her, I asked her, "Do you dislike men?" and she said, "Oh no, I do like men." She had married once and has a child about the same age as Tōru. "Whenever I fall in love with someone, I can't stop thinking about him, and would go to his house and walk

---

32 *Pachinko:* a mechanical game, similar to pinball, but smaller. It became popular after World War II.

around and around." But she gave up this sort of life entirely, and decided to live as a man.

O: I read an interview with Ms. Tsuruta written as if 'she' were a 'he.' The writer probably thought that 'she' was a man.

T: There are other funny episodes related to Ms. Tsuruta. Before leaving Japan for the first time, she was in such a hurry to take a passport photo that she wore a *haori*[33] over her suit. She asked Tōru, "Master, when I go overseas, which restroom should I use, men's or women's?" And Tōru replied seriously, "Well, Tsuruta-san, I think people will be surprised if you go into the women's restroom wearing something like that, so why don't you pretend you are a man and go into the men's room, and then use a private stall?" And she said, "That would work." We had a big laugh. When we went to the U.S. for the first time for the performance of *November Steps*, there were so many funny episodes. When Seiji Ozawa introduced *shakuhachi* player Katsuya Yokoyama and Ms. Tsuruta to the New York Philharmonic, he said, "This is Mr. Yokoyama and Mrs. Tsuruta." But somebody in the orchestra corrected him, "Seiji, your English is wrong." So from then on, he introduced them as "Mr. Yokoyama and Tsuruta-*saaan*."[34] [*laughs*]

O: If Tsuji had not introduced Ms. Tsuruta to Takemitsu, she might have remained a businesswoman. Life is unpredictable, isn't it?

T: That's right. When she started to work with Tōru, she had a lot of fun. She was truly an interesting person as a human being, and had a great deal of personality. Her life was full of up and downs.

O: I guess that shows in her *biwa* sound.

---

[33] *Haori:* Japanese formal jacket for men
[34] The honorific "—san" is gender neutral.

Takemitsu and Kinshi Tsuruta in Miyota

T: Ms. Tsuruta's *biwa* sound was something no one can imitate. Her *katari* (chanting voice) was also very good. In her later years, she sold her house and put all of her fortune into the *biwa* association.

O: When did Takemitsu first meet the *shakuhachi* player Katsuya Yokoyama?

T: I think it was for the movie *The Assassin*. Around that time, Tōru was producing a music festival called *Orchestral Space* with Toshi Ichiyanagi,[35] and he wrote *Eclipse* (1966) for *biwa* and *shakuhachi* for one of the concerts. Tōru invited Mr. Ozawa to the concert and he was extremely moved by it. I think it was owing to the sound of the *biwa* and *shakuhachi* rather than the music itself.

O: So, Mr. Ozawa told Leonard Bernstein about it?

---

[35] Toshi Ichiyanagi (1933-): Japanese composer and pianist. After studying in the United States, he returned to Japan in 1961 and introduced the music of John Cage and other radical American composers.

51

T: Yes, after Mr. Ozawa spoke with Mr. Bernstein, Tōru received a commission from the New York Philharmonic for an orchestra piece with *biwa* and *shakuhachi* for their 125th anniversary. Tōru declined at first, thinking that it was impossible. But they responded quickly, "That's fine. You don't need to use traditional Japanese instruments, so please write a piece just for the orchestra." Tōru got mad and said, "How can they make an offer and change their mind so easily?" [*laughs*] He said, "Now I will do it. The Japanese instruments don't have to fit with the orchestra. I will make their contrast more prominent."

O: That is an unknown episode in the creation of *November Steps*. It clearly shows his defiant spirit.

T: That is really true. [*laughs*]

O: So all of you, including Ms. Tsuruta and Mr. Yokoyama, went to the U.S. for the premiere of *November Steps*?

T: Yes, we all went together. Earlier, Tōru had been invited by the Rockefeller Foundation to live for one year in the United States, but he was hesitant to leave Japan since he was never able to compose abroad. So when the commission for *November Steps* arose, he asked whether he could go there at the same time as *November Steps* premiere, and they accepted his request. Maki and I also went along. Tōru traveled on the Rockefeller Foundation grant, but he didn't have to study or teach. He just went to concerts in New York, and met various people.

O: The exchange rate was fixed at 1 dollar to 360 yen, so it must have been a difficult time to travel abroad.[36]

---

[36] At present, the exchange rate is about 1 dollar to 85 yen.

At Seiji Ozawa's home in Toronto:
Front row from left: Maki Takemitsu, Seiji Ozawa.
Back row from left: Kinshi Tsuruta, skip, Takemitsu, Katsuya Yokoyama.

T: Yes it was. It was our first experience aboard an airplane. But we flew to Toronto first, not to New York. The New York Phil. was notorious for being mean to contemporary music and new pieces, so Seiji Ozawa arranged to rehearse with the Toronto Symphony Orchestra[37] first. Mr. Ozawa was in his thirties, and was already the music director for the Toronto Symphony. Unlike New York, Toronto had a warm character and Mr. Ozawa was comfortable with them, so they practiced *November Steps* with the Toronto Symphony several times. We were concerned about Ms. Tsuruta and Mr. Yokoyama facing the New York Phil. directly and being treated maliciously. So they decided to practice with the Toronto Symphony first and then go to New York. At the rehearsal with New York Phil., we heard giggles and laughs when Ms. Tsuruta and Mr. Yokoyama started playing. But at the cadenzas, they were totally fascinated and absorbed by the sonority. I

---

[37] Toronto Symphony Orchestra: founded in 1922. Seiji Ozawa assumed the position of the musical director in 1965 at the age of thirty.

think the premiere went really well. After the New York premiere, we all returned to Toronto, performed *November Steps* again, and made the first recording. In Toronto, we all stayed at Mr. Ozawa's house. I had planned to be the first one to prepare breakfast for everyone, but Mr. Ozawa always woke up when it was still dark outside, and studied scores. I could smell his coffee brewing when I woke up. That was how I learned that Mr. Ozawa was a hard worker.

O: I still have the recording of *November Steps* with the Toronto Symphony. After that, Mr. Ozawa and the Toronto Symphony came to visit Japan.

T: Yes, Ms. Tsuruta reserved an expensive Japanese restaurant in downtown Kameido and invited Mr. Ozawa, all the members of the orchestra, Tōru, Maki and myself. She told us "Master, please wear a *kimono* for the occasion." So Tōru wore *haori* and *hakama*[38] and I also wore a *kimono*. The members of Toronto Symphony were so happy to wear *yukata*.[39] The local *geisha* were there to entertain us too. Also, the *geisha* were also from downtown, so they were down-to-earth folks and lots of fun. One of the *geisha* asked Ms. Tsuruta, "Mr. President, how is your wife?" and Ms. Tsuruta said, "Ah yes, she is doing fine." [*laughs*]

O: That is so funny! I bet Ms. Tsuruta was really happy that *November Steps* was a big success. [*laughs*]

T: My daughter Maki was always calling her, "*Ojisan, ojisan* (uncle, uncle)", and she didn't mind. Yes, it is really funny. [*laughs*]

O: OK, let's go back to talking about the movies. In 1964, Takemitsu wrote at least ten film scores during that year.

T: Well, Tōru always liked composing film music—but, I didn't know that he wrote that many in 1964.

O: During the year of 1964, *Woman in the Dunes*, *The Assassin*, *Kwaidan*, *Pale Flower* ('Kawaita Hana'), *21-year-old Father* ('Nijū-issai no Chichi'),

---

[38]*Hakama*: Japanese formal attire for men.
[39]*Yukata*: Japanese informal summer wear.

The White Dawn ('Shiroi Asa'), *Japan Escape* ('Nihon Dasshutsu'),
Children hand in hand ('Te wo Tsunagu Kora'), *The Female Body* ('Nyotai'),
The Car Thief ('Jidōsha Dorobō'). They are all major works.

T: That was the time when Tōru was writing the concert piece *Textures* (1964).[40]

O: *Textures* won one of the biggest awards at that time. He must have been proud.

T: Yes, he was very proud. He received the Best Composition Award from the UNESCO International Music Council in 1965. At that time, I vomitted blood for unknown reasons and was hospitalized for three months at the Toraemon Hospital. The person next to my bed told me that there was a small article in the newspaper about the award. When Tōru came to visit with Maki, he revealed to me for that, "I had confidence in that piece." *Textures* has youth and vigor, even when I listen to it now. It is a piece I cannot forget—and it winning a big award during my hospital stay! Maki was just three years old. When she came to the hospital visiting room to see me, the first thing she'd said to me was, "I want to pee." So I held her over the toilet. But when we returned to the room, she said, "pee" again. She probably thought that the bathroom was the only place where she could be alone with me. I told her, "You shouldn't stay too long in the hospital, so you need to go home." Her father held her, and by the elevator she started to cry very loud. Well, I didn't know what to do, so now it was my turn to cry in my bed. [*laughs*] I was told by the doctor, "There is a shadow in the bronchi." I was so sure it was cancer, and decided to write a will; "Please remarry soon to somebody who cares about Maki. Don't feel bad for me. It will not be good for her without a mother." Luckily, we found out that the shadow in the bronchi was not a tumor.

O: Ah, that's why there are photos of Tōru holding Maki in the newspaper article.

---

[40] *Textures* for piano and orchestra (1964): Commissioned by NHK orchestra, and composed for the Tōkyō Olympics Art Exhibition concert.

T: Yes. After I was discharged and stayed home for a while, Tōru took Maki to Mukōgaoka Amusement Park where the azaleas were in full bloom. After she came home, Maki suddenly had a terrible asthma attack. I had rushed to her doctor's office in my nightgown.

O: Wow, I didn't know that there were so many incidents at home when Takemitsu's career was sailing along and he was presenting new works one after another. John Cage[41] visited Japan, and Takemitsu was active in the Sōgetsu Kaikan Hall.[42] In 1967 and 1968, he composed many more concert works. We could feel his vitality and his vigorous energy during these times.

T: Tōru was very busy and very energetic around that time. But instead of feeling stressed, he was enjoying it. Film music is definitely a team effort, and the creators can be inspired by one another. When working on concert pieces, it was easy to become isolated from other people, so Tōru liked to collaborate with others and become enlightened.

O: Were there many overnight sessions at the film studio?

T: Yes. Tōru went to the recording studio not only for dubbing but also for recording and mixing, and in addition to the music he was also involved in sound effects, so he did stay over a lot. But I think he did it mainly because he really loved film and he was enjoying it. He didn't come home much while he was working on *Woman in the Dunes*, but *Kwaidan* was the most challenging one. That movie was produced on a big studio set and the director Masaki Kobayashi had to sell his own house to come up with the production expenses. He lived on the second floor of a rental house until he died. Tōru had a hard time in that movie too.

O: When the movie was finished, did you go see it together?

----

[41] John Cage (1912-1992): American composer and philosopher. Cage visited Japan in 1962 and 1964. Many Japanese composers were shocked by his music, and one Japanese critic coined the phrase "Cage shock".
[42] Sōgetsu Kaikan Hall opened in 1958 by the director Hiroshi Teshigahara and became the center for much radical new art in Japan. Takemitsu took part in "Sōgetsu Music Inn" in 1961.

T: When something came up, I went to the dubbing studio and sometimes to the recording studio—but I didn't like to do that. When there was a pre-screening at Imagica in Gotanda, I always went there.

O: Before it was released?

T: Yes, and Tōru would always ask me afterwards, "So, how was it?" and that was painful.

O: You didn't like that he asked your opinion?

T: Well, it's just that I couldn't concentrate on the movie when I had to think about the music. [*laughs*]

O: You said the same thing with his concert music too.

T: So when I saw his movies, I tried to remember a few scenes. I would say, "The music for that scene was good" and "The music was nice in this other scene" Then it would sound like I was listening carefully throughout the whole movie, right? [*laughs*]

O: Exactly. You wanted to see the movie itself, not just listen to the music.

T: I don't think he wanted an expert answer, and I am not a specialist anyhow. He just wanted a response from a close friend. It was the same way when he was composing concert music. He would ask me, "I am thinking of doing this, but what do you think?"

O: Did you usually compliment him?

T: Yes, of course I did—but only on the good parts. I would say, "That part was good." It is strange that I say this, but I have to say I didn't understand much of his concert music—but his film music is really great. He had specific ideas about which instruments would work for which movie, and what kind of sound was suitable. I thought it was amazing to have such ideas, like using prepared piano[43] for *The Pitfall*. I never said it in front of Tōru, but he did have talent for film music! [*laughs*].

O: Sometimes he composed music that was not entirely synchronized with, but rather slightly off from the image on the screen, and it clearly made the movie come alive. There were times when I saw a movie and was impressed with the music, and found out later that it was written by Takemitsu. The opening scene of *Double Suicide* (1969) is unforgettable. It starts out when the director Shinoda makes a phone call, and suddenly we hear Gamelan music. It is so unforgettable.

T: *Double Suicide* is a good movie, isn't it? I think that is one of the best scores Tōru undertook in collaboration with director Mr. Shinoda. Tōru did have a keen sense for determining exactly when to use the music in movies—but please don't say that Takemitsu's wife was praising his film music. [*laughs*]

O: I guess those are the true feelings of Tōru's eternal movie comrade. Takemitsu's film music was really written as if he were staking his life on it.

T: For the first ten years—that was a period when his film music was made with care and time. It was a good time. But the composing fees were not that good. Film music budgets were pre-determined, and studios had to manage their expenses. Tōru wanted to hire good performers, and that cut into his composition fee.

O: I heard that when Takemitsu went to the U.S., people thought he was a millionaire after finding out that he was writing so much film music.

T: When he went to L.A. and said he wrote music for about ninety films, people—after finding out that he wrote so much film music— thought he was really rich. At the news conference, Tōru was asked, "How many pools do you have in your house?" and he answered, "I

---

[43] Prepared piano: a modified piano invented by John Cage. Objects, such as erasers, felt, and screws are inserted on or between the strings and hammers.

only have one small bathtub in my house."—they thought he was joking. But it was true! [*laughs*] There were several films which failed to make money, so he could not get paid, but Tōru really liked composing film music so he said it was OK. Anyway, that was a good period for Japanese films. In later years, the Japanese film industry fell into financial strains, and Tōru didn't have opportunities to write the sort of film music that he loved so much. He looked a little sad...

Takemitsu in his home in Shibuya, Tōkyō. 1970   ©Bunyō Ishikawa

Chapter 3

Takemitsu's Debut until 'Music Today'

Chapter 3 begins with a brief glance at Takemitsu's passion for baseball and his infatuation for the Ōsaka-based *Hanshin Tigers*, a quirky team with a fanatic and enthusiastic fan base. The interview then turns to cover the early years of Takemitsu's career, and the importance of individual performers (such as Yūji Takahashi, Peter Serkin, and Kiyoshi Shōmura) to the types of works Takemitsu composed and the stylistic directions that he explored. The interview concludes by discussing *Music Today*, a contemporary music festival in Tōkyō that Takemitsu ran for twenty years. Tucked inside these brief portraits and vignettes are striking revelations regarding Takemitsu's understanding of the relationship of music and society, and the role that music might play in constructing a better world.

A Big Fan of Hanshin Tigers

O'hara: Takemitsu was a huge fan of the Hanshin Tigers,[1] wasn't he? This year, Hanshin is in great shape (Hanshin won the league championship in 2003). When I went to visit your home in Miyota, I was so surprised to find photos and articles related to Hanshin winning the Japanese title in 1985. Did Takemitsu's loyalty extend back to before you were married?

Takemitsu: Oh yes, since his childhood—when Fujimura[2] was still with Hanshin.

O: Since his childhood? But he grew up in Tōkyō (where Hanshin's rival, the Yomiuri Giants, is the home team).

T: Yes, he was in Tōkyō, but I guess he needed to go against something. So if he were in Ōsaka, maybe he would have become a Yomiuri Giants[3] fan. Umm, maybe not. [*laughs*]

O: So he didn't like that the majority was rooting for the Giants. He had a defiant attitude toward authority.

T: That's right. He didn't like 'goody-goody' like the Giants. Hanshin was sort of a team that could win even after getting drunk the night before. Tōru liked that kind of spontaneous spirit. [*laughs*]

O: Are you a Hanshin fan too?

T: My parents had connections in Kyūshū, so they were Seitetsu Lions fans, and so was I. I don't remember when I became a Hanshin fan. By

---

[1] Hanshin Tigers: A Japanese professional baseball team based in Ōsaka. They won the league championship in 2003 for the first time in eighteen years. This interview was held during the season when the Tigers were leading with a wide margin.
[2] Tomio Fujimura (1916-92): joined the Ōsaka Tigers in 1951 and was inducted into the Baseball Hall of Fame in 1974. He had a successful career as both a pitcher and a batter; his nickname was 'Mr. Tigers.'
[3] Yomiuri Giants: One of the most popular Japanese professional baseball team based in Tōkyō. They are regarded as "The New York Yankees of Japan."

the time Maki was in elementary school, we were all Hanshin fans. She even kept a baseball diary of Hanshin's game results. This is when Tabuchi and Enatsu[4] were still there. Hanshin was very strong back then.

O: Sometime ago, I found a newspaper interview with Takemitsu when he won the Japan Academy Prize for film music. He said, "Movies aside—I want to mention that our family wrote a protest letter to the president of the Hanshin Tigers team about the trading of Tabuchi. All three of our family members have signed our names in protest." [*laughs*] He was a Tigers fan through and through.

T: At that time, he was furious about Enatsu's trade. If he were still alive, this year would have been tough. [*laughs*]

O: I heard that there was something called *Meikyū-kai*, where a bunch of musicians placed bets on which team would win that year. Shinichirō Ikebe, Hiroshi Koizumi,[5] and Sumire Yoshihara were members, right?

T: Mr. Ikebe and Mr. Koizumi bet on Hiroshima Carp; Tōru, Maki and I bet on Hanshin Tigers; the husband and wife Yasunori Yamaguchi[6] and Sumire Yoshihara bet on Yakult Swallows. Even after Tōru and Kuniharu Akiyama died, the group continued on for eighteen years. The fan of the winning team was supposed to treat the rest of the members to dinner. But as nobody won, the betting pool grew larger and larger. So after the fifth season, we all decided to use the money for a trip.

O: Everybody bet on their favorite team. So no one could win. [*laughs*]

T: Even when the Giants were overpowering the other teams, winning championships for nine consecutive years, Tōru would not bet on the

---

4 Kōichi Tabuchi was a catcher and Yutaka Enatsu was a pitcher. They formed a battery during the 1970s.
5 Hiroshi Koizumi (1944-): Japanese flutist. He premiered Takemitsu's *Le Fils des Etoiles* (1975), and *Toward the Sea* (1981).
6 Yasunori Yamaguchi and Sumire Yoshihara: percussionists. They premiered Takemitsu's *Rain Tree*(1981) and performed in many film scores by Takemitsu.

Giants. [*laughs*] Tōru's father used to be an umpire for the Tōkyō Big Six University Baseball League at the Jingū Stadium, so it might be in his blood. [*laughs*]

Takemitsu's Debut

O: OK, let's get back to the business. [*laughs*] In our first interview, you said that you went to the premiere of Takemitsu's debut piece, *Lento in Due Movimenti* for solo piano (1950).

T: Yes, I think it was at Yomiuri Hall in Yūrakuchō, Tōkyō. Tōru gave me a ticket and I went with my elder sister.

O: Do you remember anything about the concert? Were you sitting next to Takemitsu? Was there a large audience?

T: Hmm, it was more than fifty years ago. I don't remember much.

O: Did you talk to Takemitsu after the concert?

T: Not much. We weren't that close at the time. It was totally different than a normal classical music concert. The 'newness' made an impact on me, but I don't recollect that we talked about it.

O: *Lento in Due Movimenti* was criticized by Ginji Yamane with the famous line, "It is pre-music."[7] Did Takemitsu talk about that later on?

T: *Lento in Due Movimenti* was criticized as 'pre-music,' and someone else complained that 'there is something wrong with him placing two *Lento* movements in a row. It is like putting *shiruko* and *zenzai* (two similar *azuki*-bean soups) side by side. [*laughs*] Tōru was shocked at that time, but he didn't drag it out too long. What's done is done. This was his debut concert, and he didn't know whether he could be successful as a composer. I think the criticism bothered him a little, but he was happy that he met Kuniharu Akiyama and Jōji Yuasa who were moved

---

[7] Yamane's review appeared in the *Tōkyō Shinbun*, December 12, 1950.

by his music and who came to see him in the greenroom after the concert.

O: The score of *Lento in Due Movimenti* was lost afterwards.

T: Tōru didn't hold onto his belongings very well. It seems that the score was kept by his composer friend Kazuo Fukushima.[8]

O: In 1989, Takemitsu composed *Litany*, basing it on *Lento in Due Movimenti*.

T: Yes, but Tōru didn't recover the score from Mr. Fukushima. He found a recording of *Lento in Due Movimenti* and re-composed it after listening to the recording.

O: The NHK broadcast station holds a tape recording of *Lento in Due Movimenti* performed by Takahiro Sonoda,[9] but only the second *Lento* of the two exists. It was recorded in 1957, seven years after it was composed.

T: I wonder why the score was at Mr. Fukushima's place.

O: I heard that Fukushima's elder sister Hideko kept it.

T: Maybe it was something having to do with *Jikken Kōbō*, and Tōru gave it to Ms. Hideko? After the concert was over, probably thought it was OK to give it away.

O: After *Lento in Due Movimenti*, Takemitsu wrote *Distance de Fée* for violin and piano (1951/89).

T: He heard that the violinist Akiko Suwa—the younger sister of the famed violinist Nejiko Suwa—was interested in contemporary music.

---

[8] Kazuo Fukushima(1930-): composer, musicologist. In 1946, at the age of sixteen, he met Takemitsu in a choir. He joined *Jikken Kōbō* in 1952.
[9] Takahiro Sonoda (1928-2004): pianist. He premiered Takemitsu's second piano work *Uninterrupted Rest* on August 9, 1952 at *Jikken Kōbō*'s fourth concert. He introduced works by many contemporary composers, including Gershwin, Khachaturian, and Messiaen, to the Japanese public.

So he, along with Kuniharu Akiyama, paid her a visit and asked her to play *Distance de Fée*.

O: How interesting. He visited Ms. Suwa's house.

T: For the premiere, the piano part was played by Haruko Fujita, wasn't it?

O: Yes, it was Haruko Fujita. Then after *Distance de Fée* came *Uninterrupted Rest* (1952-59).

T: I've forgotten who played the premiere.

O: Part I was performed by Takahiro Sonoda, and Part II and Part III were performed by Haruko Kasama.

T: I went to Mr. Sonoda's premiere at the lecture hall of Women's College in Ichigaya, Tōkyō. Several artists participated in this *Jikken Kōbō*'s concert, and Shōzō Kitadai's mobile was on display. During the second *Jikken Kōbō* concert, which was held at the same hall, there was a big earthquake that shook the entire building.

O: During the performance?

T: Yes, it was during the Japanese premiere of Messiaen's *Quartet for the End of Time*. [*laughs*]

O: So, everyone really thought it was the end of the world! [*laughs*]

T: The mobile was shaking very hard, and soon it was spinning around and around above the stage as if it could crash any time. [*laughs*] It was an unforgettable concert.

O: *Uninterrupted Rest* Part I was composed in 1952, and Parts II and III were composed in 1959. *Requiem for Strings* was composed in 1957 so it must have been a little before that. Around that time, Takemitsu also started composing for film music and tape music. It was when his film was garnering attention. The piece that premiered the year after *Requiem for Strings* was *Le Son Calligraphié*.

T: When was the premiere of *Le Son Calligraphié*?

O: Part I and Part II were in 1958, and Part III was in 1960. Part I was premiered at the Second Contemporary Music Festival presented by the Twentieth-Century Music Society in August 1958. Part II was premiered at the Tōkyō Yamaha Hall in November 1958; Part III was at Sōgetsu Hall in Tōkyō in April 1960.

T: Talking about *Le Son Calligraphié*, there was an international radio center called KRC in Akasaka, Tōkyō. The location was near Sōgetsu Hall, down the street from the Canadian Embassy. Tōru recorded there often and later made the musique concrète[10] *Quiet Design* (1960) there. Naosumi Yamamoto conducted *Le Son Calligraphié* and I went to listen to it.

O: Was it a rehearsal or a recording session?

T: I don't remember the occasion, but I do remember that Tōru was really impressed with him and said, "Naosumi is great. He is a genius at conducting. He can read this kind of score at sight."

O: Two years after this piece, in December 1960, Takemitsu returned to Tōkyō from Kamakura. Was Takemitsu about thirty years old?

T: Yes, he composed *Solitude Sonore* (1958) around that time. Tōru lived in Kamakura between the age of twenty-five and thirty, then moved to Tōkyō in 1960, and composed *Music of Trees* in 1961. At the end of that year, our daughter was born, so we named her *Ma-ki* ('real tree'). He said that she ought to be a real tree and wanted her to grow vigorously like a tree. I didn't like my own name, so I wanted to name her something that ends with 'ko.'[11]

---

[10] musique concrète: an early form of electronic music utilizing sounds recorded from 'real' life.

[11] —ko: a common ending in Japanese for many girl names (Masako, Tomoko, Mitsuko, etc.).

Yūji Takahashi

O: During 1961, Takemitsu composed *Piano Distance*, which was dedicated to Yūji Takahashi.[12] When did you meet Takahashi for the first time?

T: When we still lived in Kamakura, we were on a train on the Yokosuka Line and saw a man who had emanated a very different atmosphere from the others.

O: That was Takahashi?

T: Yes, he was wearing flip-flops that you normally wear at the beach. He was not that shabby, but kind of odd looking. He wasn't sitting even though there was a vacant seat; instead, he was leaning against the door. He had some kind of special aura, which made him stand out in a crowd. So Tōru and I were wondering what this man did for a living.

O: All of you were still young.

T: Yes, young! I think we were about seventeen or eighteen years old. Yūji was probably still in high school, and he was really handsome. So we were attending a contemporary music concert at the Bridgestone Museum in Kyōbashi, Tōkyō— *Jikken Kōbō* sometimes had concerts there too—when suddenly we spotted the same young man on the Yokosuka Line standing at the back of the hall. So I said, "Tōru-san, there's that man. If he's at this kind of concert, then maybe he's a music-related person." We didn't know Yūji just yet.

O: Was that the first encounter? That is so funny. I met Takahashi the other day and asked him where you all first met, and he said on the Yokosuka Line. He thought, "There is an odd man. It must be Takemitsu!"

---

[12] Yūji Takahashi (1938 -): composer and pianist. Takemitsu dedicated *Piano Distance* (1961) and *Asterism* (1968) to Takahashi. Takahashi also collaborated with Takemitsu on the film scores *The Pitfall* (Otoshiana, 1962) and *Pale Flower* ('Kawaita Hana' 1964).

T: Really? I never heard about that. I didn't know he was thinking about the same thing. [*laughs*]

O: You usually see the same people at contemporary music concerts, and people who had to travel as far as Kamakura would be on the same train to and from Tōkyō. So it was easy for Takahashi to identify Takemitsu.

T: Yūji's first wife Utako Akimoto grew up close to my house and Tōru's house in Setagaya-Daita. Tōru remembered her as a little girl riding on a tricycle. She was very smart and cute. Utako graduated from Tōkyō National University of Fine Arts and Music as a composition major. She met Yūji and got married in 1957 or 1958. They rented an apartment on a second floor near the Nisseki Hospital in Azabu, Tōkyō. Once she asked us to come over, Tōru and I visited them. Yūji was out at work, and later we heard him panting as he hurried up the stairs. It was so heart-warming to see that. They were like children playing house. Tōru and I were so poor and still recovering from illness, so there was nothing romantic about us. Yūji and Tōru became very close around that time, and Tōru was attracted not only to Yūji's piano playing but also to his personality. They visited each other's home frequently. Right after Yūji received a scholarship from the Rockefeller Foundation to live in the United States, we were likewise invited by the Rockefeller Foundation and stayed in New York for a while. We went to Japanese and Chinese restaurants together in New York. But a while later, Tōru and Yūji gradually drifted apart, and Yūji wrote essays critical of Tōru's way of life and work.

O: That was when the so-called 'Political Season' arrived in the late 1960's.[13]

T: I think Tōru was shocked when Yūji criticized him. Tōru thought it was fun when Ryūichi Sakamoto[14] gave out pamphlets criticizing Tōru and other younger people doing certain things.

---

[13] 'Political Season': a period when younger Japanese became involved in politics and demonstrated against the Vietnam War and other social issues.

[14] Ryūichi Sakamoto (1952-): composer. He played a leading part in techno-pop music. In 1970, Sakamoto was a student at Tōkyō National University of Fine Arts and Music, and he protested against Takemitsu's music.

O: Takemitsu was a close friend of Takahashi, so he must have been in deep shock.

T: Tōru appreciated Yūji's piano playing very much, so I think he was hurt. After a long period of estrangement, Tōru came home one day looking very cheerful and said to me, "Today, Yūji said hello." Don't you think the whole thing was pitiful? [*laughs*]

O: I asked Takahashi about this incident the other day to get his side of the story. Takemitsu was doing a book signing of a new score. Takahashi already had the score in possession, but bought it again and lined up at the end of the queue. After giving an autograph, Takemitsu looked up and said, "Oh, Yūji!" That was their reunion after more than ten years. Takahashi said, "Takemitsu said 'Let's go have some tea,' so we went together." Takahashi was probably referring to the same day that Tōru came home in a good mood.

Yuji Takahashi playing Takemitsu's early piano work. 2004.

T: Even though they hadn't seen each other for a long time, Tōru always cared and often thought about him.

O: It seems that Takahashi was also thinking about him and said, "I shouldn't have written so harshly about Takemitsu back then, but I was also young…"[15]

T: When Tōru and Yūji were good friends, they weren't the type of people who argued. When I look at their relationship, they were rather quiet people, so Tōru didn't know why Yūji suddenly turned his back on Tōru. It would've been acceptable if Yūji was criticizing Tōru's compositions or musical things, but Yūji was criticizing his way of living…Tōru always said having only a handful of friends he could rely on would be enough for him. In other words, he was trying to stay loyal to his friends. And of course Yūji was one of Tōru's friends, so I think Tōru was upset for a while.

O: Since Takemitsu's passing, I have listened to Takahashi's performance of Takemitsu's compositions several times.

T: Yūji's playing is different from others.

O: In our *Complete Takemitsu Edition* project, we asked Takahashi to record *Two Melodies* (1948) and other study pieces by then seventeen-year-old Takemitsu. The performances are very good.

T: Yūji is a remarkable person. I have also listened to that recording session, and it is truly marvelous.

O: In the recording session, you two were talking over something quite interesting in the green room.

T: When I saw Yūji playing the piano, he resembled Tōru from behind. When I told him, he said "There is a gesture of a sound. It is like the composer's body gradually floating to the surface as in a photo negative." And I thought, "That's it!"

---

[15] In the 1970s, Takahashi advocated that musicians participate in social movements, but Takemitsu was against it.

O: I had deep emotions upon hearing Takahashi performing Takemitsu's study pieces, even the newly discovered ones.

Encounter with the performers

O: Takemitsu often dedicated his compositions to the performers with whom he worked.

T: Early on, he did have a favorite instrument, such as guitar or flute. And since Tōru didn't study at a music conservatory, whenever he encountered an instrument that he wasn't familiar with, he was surprised to learn, "Wow, this instrument can do such a thing!" I think it often happened when he met outstanding performers.

O: For example, Yūji Takahashi, Peter Serkin,[16] and Richard Stoltzman.[17]

T: Tōru wasn't so interested in clarinet at first, but he came to like it after meeting Stoltzman. Whenever he met great performers, such as oboist Heinz Holliger,[18] violist Nobuko Imai, and trombonist Vinko Globokar,[19] Tōru wanted to compose for them. So his real motivation for composing was his encounter with these eminent people. And the funny thing is that Tōru became friends with these performers quite easily—even in Canada with flutist Robert Aitken[20] and percussionist John Wyre and the members of Nexus.

O: When was his first encounter with Robin Engelman and John Wyre who premiered *Bryce* (1976)?

---

[16] Peter Serkin (1947-): American pianist, son of the renowned pianist Rudolf Serkin. Takemitsu dedicated *riverrun* (1984), and *Les yeux clos II* (1988) to Peter.

[17] Richard Stoltzman (1942-): American clarinetist. Takemitsu dedicated several pieces to him including *Waves* (1976), and *Fantasma/Cantos* (1991).

[18] Heinz Holliger (1939-): Swiss oboist. Takemitsu dedicated *Distance* (1972) to him.

[19] Vinko Globokar (1934-): Yugoslavian trombonist. Takemitsu composed *Gémeaux* (1971-86) with Globokar in mind as the trombonist.

[20] Robert Aitken (1939-): Canadian flutist. He premiered *Bryce* (1976), and *Toward the Sea—Part I: The Night* (1981).

T: They met in Toronto. Both Engelman and Wyre still performed with the Toronto Symphony back then.

O: As orchestral members?

T: Yes, but they quit the orchestra one day, and formed a group by themselves. They were introduced to Tōru by Seiji Ozawa. Mr. Ozawa said, "I don't know why, but everyone becomes a Takemitsu fanatic. They think he is mysterious, but actually he is not. Still everyone joins the Takemitsu cult." [*laughs*] I think it was better that we met in Canada instead of New York. Canadian people can be more liberal, and Canada as a country accepted exiles and refugees. The next time we visited Canada was during the Vietnam War, and we found many Americans who dodged the military draft and crossed the border into Canada. They were generous to foreigners, and there were a lot of Chinese immigrants too.

O: When did Takemitsu meet Peter Serkin, son of the great pianist Rudolf Serkin?

T: After *November Steps*, the Toronto Symphony and Yūji Takahashi recorded *Asterism* (1968) conducted by Seiji Ozawa in 1969. At the recording session, Peter was listening in the auditorium. I think Mr. Ozawa told us that he was Rudolf Serkin's son and then Tōru and Peter started talking to each other. But Peter was tired of people saying he was the son of Rudolf Serkin. He was a vagabond for a while, and did yoga and lived like a hippie.

O: That was when he had long hair.

T: Yes, he had his long hair put up in the back. Tōru and Peter didn't get the chance to talk much when they first met, but they reconnected several years later at the *Marlboro Music Festival*.

O: That was when Casals led the *Marlboro Festival*.

Takemitsu and Stoltzman. ca. 1990.

T: Yes, Peter still had long hair put up in a pony tail, and practiced yoga, sitting cross-legged on the lawn. He was always talking about eating brown rice or something like that. When he played Tōru's piano pieces, Tōru said to him, "Well, if you only eat vegetables, you won't have much strength. I think you'd better eat meat, too." And so Peter started eating meat! [*laughs*] When people from the East say something, Westerns think of it as something mysterious. Mr. Ozawa used to laugh at Peter saying that he was a disciple of the Takemitsu cult. We used to go hiking and went for a ride together with his first wife Wendy, their baby, and their dog named Tashi. I don't remember the meaning of Tashi.

O: It means 'good fortune' in Tibetan.

T: That's right! One time, with their dog named 'Good Fortune,' the three of us and the three of them went hiking together, bringing along picnic sandwiches. Then we arrived at this prairie as big as the eye could see, and we stopped by an old mansion. That mansion belonged to Rudolf Serkin. At that time, Rudolf Serkin was like God to us.

Peter's father was absent, but his sister and a cat were there. There were some old photos hanging on the wall, and the room had a silent, dignified atmosphere, like in the movies. I remember Tōru standing in front of the piano and pondering something.

O: Takemitsu composed many pieces for Peter.

T: Tōru said Peter's sound is very transparent and intellectual.

O: I agree. When I listened to his Mozart Piano Concerto No. 17 and No.19—Peter's debut recording—I was impressed with the clarity of the notes and the pure tone. It is a refreshing performance.

T: Tōru said Peter's tone quality suited his own music very well. So he liked the performances of Peter's group Tashi as well. Ida Kavafian's violin playing was very beautiful, but occasionally she made her instrument sing too much, and it sounded like a gypsy violin. So Tōru told her, "Hold back, hold back." [*laughs*]

Members of Tashi: from left; Richard Stoltzman, Peter Serkin, Takemitsu, Ida Kavafian, and Fred Sherry. 1977.   ©Akira KINOSHITA

O: Tōru met Nobuko Imai at the *Aldeburgh Festival* when she performed Britten.

T: I think that was the first time he heard her perform live. After meeting Ms. Imai, he became fascinated by the viola, and then he composed *A String Around Autumn* (1989). It was a similar situation to when he composed *From me flows what you call Time* (1990) after meeting the members of Nexus. It was always like that.

O: Takemitsu was good friends with conductor and composer Oliver Knussen.[21]

T: When we stayed in London for the *Aldeburgh Festival*, I think we first met Ollie (Oliver) at the Schott music store. They immediately got along as if they had known each other for a long time. They were talking about movies and joking around. I guess they really hit it off.

O: I heard that the encounter with the guitarist Kiyoshi Shōmura was funny. You first saw him on TV?

T: Yes, Maki and I were surfing channels on TV and came upon Mr. Shōmura, who was very handsome. He didn't look so tender and gentle like today, but more wild.

O: Ah, that's right. When he was young, he had a long hair—black as ebony.

T: Tōru was fond of the guitar, but he didn't know many classical guitarists. He knew jazz or popular guitarists like Harumi Ibe, and asked Mr. Ibe to play lute for his composition *RING* (1961).

O: At that time, there weren't many serious classical guitarists and lute players in Japan.

---

[21] Oliver Knussen (1952-): composer and conductor. He conducted the premieres of Takemitsu's *Rain Coming* (1982), *Tree Line* (1988), and *Archipelago S.* (1993). He invited Takemitsu to *Tanglewood Festival* in 1986 and the *Aldeburgh Festival* in 1993.

T: We found Mr. Shōmura on TV after he returned to Japan from his studies in Spain. Tōru and I were impressed and said, "Wow, he is really good." Then after a week or so, we received a phone call from him saying, "My name is Shōmura. I play the guitar and just came back from Spain. I would like to ask you to write a piece for me." I told Maki, "He's the guy we saw on TV—the good-looking guy!" [*laughs*] But I totally forgot what day he planned to visit our house. And when the doorbell rang that morning, I went to get the door in a hurry. My hair was totally messy, but there he was! I was in panic! [*laughs*] How long ago was that? It is more than thirty years ago.

O: Yes, Shōmura said his recording debut was thirty-five years ago, so that meeting should've been at least thirty years ago. Where did you live at that time?

T: We lived in an apartment next to the NHK studio in Shibuya. One time, Mr. Shōmura was with us and the topic turned to baseball. When he said, "I am a Giants fan," Tōru said jokingly, "I am not composing for you." [*laughs*] Then Mr. Shōmura replied, "Well, I can become a Hanshin fan." [*laughs*] He was a real Giants fanatic, so I couldn't believe he would say that. [*laughs*]

O: I heard that Mr. Takemitsu asked Mr. Shōmura about the guitar's capabilities.

T: He learned so many things from Mr. Shōmura about the nature of the instrument and its potentials. Tōru had been fond of the guitar for a long time, but he didn't know much about fingering and other complicated matters. He really appreciated Mr. Shōmura and said that he was his guitar teacher.

O: Did Takemitsu play the guitar?

T: No, I don't think you can say that he could really 'play' it.

O: Shōmura said Takemitsu's music didn't have any unnecessary notes, so it was difficult and there was no way to cheat.

T: Tōru didn't know much about the guitar, so he would ask Mr. Shōmura if it's possible to do a certain technique, and Mr. Shōmura would say, "I can try, it should be fine." So I guess the music turned out to be difficult.

O: There are several works dedicated to Shōmura: *Folios* (1974), *Equinox* (1993), *Rosedale* from *In the Woods* (1995), and *Twelve Songs for Guitar* (1974 – 77), and so forth. Among these works, *Twelve Songs for Guitar* has a slightly different flavor to it. How did he select the twelve songs for transcription?

T: It was difficult to choose these twelve songs. There were a few songs that he was uncertain about, and he discussed it with me. Since the rest were mostly foreign songs, I suggested *A Song of Early Spring* ('Sōshunfu').[22] It was a song that not many were familiar with, and even Shuntarō Tanikawa said he didn't know the song. *Londonderry Air* was simple but a good song, so I suggested he include it. The hymn *What a Friend We Have in Jesus* was effectively used in the British movie *O Lucky Man!* It made a strong impression on me, so I suggested this song as well. So I was quite involved with the selection of *Twelve Songs for Guitar.*

O: *The International*[23] is also included.

T: That selection was by Tōru. He said that the melody is really beautiful. But it was a 'Union' song in Japan, and he didn't like the impression of "Arise, you prisoners of starvation…" He said that, "When you listen to that melody, it needs to be more tuneful and should make people happier, rather than just be sung as a labor song." He wrote the transcription to counter the feeling of the original version of *The International.*

O: He included three romantic Beatles songs in the set, and *The International* is a really beautiful transcription. Mr. Shōmura lived in

---

[22] *Sōshunfu*: A Japanese song from the late 19th century composed by Akira Nakata
[23] *The International* became the anthem of international socialism, and was prominent in the Soviet Union until the mid-1940s. Charles Hope Kerr authored an English version, which begins: "Arise, you prisoners of starvation! Arise, you wretched of the earth! For justice thunders condemnation: A better world's in birth!"

Spain between the ages of sixteen and twenty, so he didn't know that *The International* was a protest song, and didn't know the meaning of the lyrics either. Because of this, he didn't try to capture the meaning of the original version—so it seems more romantic when Mr. Shōmura is playing.

T: He didn't know the meaning? When members of our generation listen to this song, it evokes a distinct feeling, apart from the fact that the melody is beautiful. But instead of pouring out the emotion forcefully, the melody can soar quietly. That's why I think it is still beautiful even though I know it's a worker's protest song.

O: Takemitsu felt *The International* was romantic in nature, and I think his idea of it was quite different from that of the radical musicians, such as Ryūichi Sakamoto and Yūji Takahashi. But the basic idea and the ultimate goal of politics should be living a peaceful life and to be romantic. So I think Takemitsu's point of view was different from those other musicians.

T: That is right. He was conscious about that, and said that we should not be ignorant about society and politics. Living in the present means we are related to those things. But he didn't want to speak out too loudly. That's why I think he wanted to appeal to people by transcribing the labor song *The International* as quiet and beautiful music with lots of heart.

O: But the young people in the 60s and 70s were more radical and spoke out loudly.

T: Yes, that's right—young people back then.

O: They were alienated from the society. It was that kind of period.

Year of composition

O: When we were compiling the *Complete Takemitsu Edition*, there were many disagreements about the year that certain works were composed.

We assembled them in order according to the year of composition, so we needed to figure out which versions came out first.

T: Which ones, for example?

O: There are three versions of *Toward the Sea*. The first one is for alto-flute and guitar; the next is for alto-flute, harp, and string orchestra; the third for alto-flute and harp without the string orchestra. Incidently, this last version was premiered by harpist Mari Kimura five years before the score was published. But officially, the year of publication is listed as the year that it was composed.

T: I see. I think Mari helped to sort out the chronology in regards to *Toward the Sea II*. Tōru should have been involved at some level and they might have corresponded with each other. Later Tōru published *Toward the Sea III*. So I think it is fine to list the year of composition as the publication date.

O: Yes, we also listed it in the collection that way. There is another interesting example. The world premiere of *Rain Tree Sketch II*[24] for solo piano, was officially listed as Alain Neveux at Messeiaen's tribute concert in France. But we discovered later that Aki Takahashi performed it in Japan slightly earlier due to the time difference.

T: Really, Aki played it earlier…?

O: The performance in France was at Messiaen's tribute concert, so they listed it as a 'World Premiere,' and Ms. Takahashi's concert program says 'Japanese Premiere.' In reality, the 'Japanese Premiere' came before the 'World Premiere.' [*laughs*]

T: So many small things to consider in order to compile an entire collection! [*laughs*] There is also a debate about which one of the two is Takemitsu's very last work—*Air*[25] or *In the Woods*.[26] Tōru wrote these pieces simultaneously, so it is hard to say.

---

[24] *Rain Tree Sketch II*: composed in memoriam to Olivier Messiaen (1992).
[25] *Air* for solo flute (1995) was premiered on January 28, 1996. In Japan, flutist Hiroshi Koizumi performed this piece at Takemitsu's funeral on Feb. 29, 1996.

O: Generally, *Air* is considered a posthumous work.

T: As I recall, after *Air* was completed, the score was sent to Switzerland, and it was several days before the premiere. Tōru was working on the guitar pieces *In the Woods* until the very end, so I think *In the Woods* is the last piece. Still, everyone claims that *Air* is the posthumous work.

O: In our research, we also found that *In the Woods* was written after *Air*.

T: If it's according to the order of the compositions, I think so. *Air* was written in honor of Mr. Nicole, on his seventieth birthday, but *In the Woods* was not written for a commission, but was for Tōru's own pleasure. So I think after he completed *Air*, he focused on *In the Woods*. *In the Woods* contains three pieces, and Mr. Shōmura was involved throughout the process, so I am sure it was written later. Tōru was discharged from the hospital in October, and he composed only these pieces between October and December. He was writing both works simultaneously, so it shouldn't really matter which one is the 'posthumous' work.

O: That's right.

T: If everyone says *Air* is Tōru's last work, it is fine with me. It doesn't mean much whether one was finished earlier or later. When was the premiere of *Air*?

O: *Air* was premiered on January 28th, 1996.

T: Oh, it was January. After completing *In the Woods*, he started working on *Comme la sculpture de Miró*. If he had managed to finish it, *Miró* would have been a posthumous work.

---

26 *In the Woods* (1995): these three pieces for guitar were inspired by different woods: "Wainscot Pond"— after a painting by Cornelia Foss—is dedicated to John Williams; "Rosedale" is dedicated to Kiyoshi Shōmura; and "Muir Woods" is for Julian Bream.

O: Do you know if the guitar work *In the Woods* was inspired by anything in particular?

T: It had to do with an event that happened one year before he passed away. We were visiting San Francisco, and Peter Grilli[27] took us into the woods in the suburbs. There was a huge Sequoia tree. Tōru crawled into the cavern beneath it, and Peter took some photos. We had dinner at a restaurant afterwards, and Peter forgot his camera there. He had taken so many good photos that everyone was disappointed. [*laughs*] I think that the woods made a deep impression on Tōru and decided to compose this piece after returning to Japan.

O: I heard that he could compose chamber music rather quickly.

T: Orchestral music took a lot of effort, but there were many chamber works he wanted to compose. It is said that Takemitsu's orchestral works possess a certain characteristic tone colors and use a unique orchestration. When *A String Around Autumn* was premiered in Paris, Messiaen was in the audience and praised his orchestration. But Tōru used to say, "I always have doubts about being known as an orchestral composer."

O: Really?

T: Another issue that concerned him was whether the orchestra as a form fits with our present society. Tens of hundreds of performers need to be hired, and unless someone is willing to support it financially, it is difficult to make the performance happen. And even if it is performed, only limited number of audience members can listen to it. You can listen to a CD at home, but a live performance is a different experience. So there are many problems in hand. Tōru said that he had many things he wanted to do with an orchestra. While it was possible to write these things for an orchestra, he said his style might be more suitable for smaller ensembles. Maybe I shouldn't say this, but Tōru used to say, "If it's for chamber ensemble, I can write it instantly."

---

[27] Peter Grilli (1942-): American producer, the President of Japan Society of Boston. He produced Takemitsu's documentary movie *Dream/Window* (1992), and *Music for the Movies* (1994).

What he meant by 'instantly' is not that he thought it was easy, but that he had particular ideas about how to write for certain instruments, so that he thought he could compose as many works as possible. He also said this is somewhat scary because he might just dash something off without thinking. I remember him saying that two or three years before he died.

O: But he had many commissions for a large scale orchestra.

T: Yes, many commissions were for orchestras and there was one for an opera. People might have thought that he was arrogant, but he used to say, "There are many small pieces I want to write and I can write as many as I want. If it is for orchestra, it's not that easy."

O: Do you know if the unfinished work *Comme la sculpture de Miró* was supposed to be a concerto for flute and harp?

T: Yes, but his draft stops before the flute and harp enter.

O: That is such a pity.

T: There was an exhibition of Miró's paintings and sculptures at the Musée d'art Mercian in Karuizawa that Takemitsu went to see between October and December, after he was discharged from the hospital. The sculptures were constructed with tools for daily use. It was such an ingenuous exhibit.

O: They were made out of brooms, rakes, and shovels and things like that.

T: Yes, it was simple but sophisticated, yet ingenuous and full of energy. Tōru's cancer was in remission and he was back to Miyota at that time after his illness and hospitalization. So he was truly moved to see that kind of vitality and joy of life in Miró's sculptures. He went to see the exhibit so many times, and whenever friends visited, he would ask them to go together. He told everyone about it as if it were his own exhibit. He was so impressed with Miró's sculptures that he decided to write his 'last' piece.

O: I see.

T: I wish that he had progressed a little farther though…

O: It is really a pity. I wish we could listen to this work for flute and harp.

T: And Tōru wanted to have Milva[28] sing in his opera.[29] But perhaps Milva is not suitable for operatic singing, don't you think?

O: Well, I don't know. Maybe Milva's operatic voice might actually be good though. Speaking of singing, Takemitsu didn't produce many vocal works.

T: He didn't write many songs in general. Tōru said songs are difficult. Even if the poem is good, it can be hard to set a melody to it. For example, the meaning of 'a-shi'[30] will be different depending upon how you set it to a melody. He said that was strange.

O: That's right. The meaning will be different depending upon whether the intonation is high or low.

T: Japanese accents are about high or low, not strong or weak, so it was hard for him to set Japanese words to music. The chanting of Japanese traditional ballads, such as *gidayū*[31] or *naniwa-bushi*,[32] is better in sync with the Japanese language. So, it is funny to hear Japanese versions of Western operas, isn't it?

---

[28] Milva (1939-): Italian singer, actress, and TV personality.

[29] Takemitsu's opera was commissioned by the Opéra National de Lyon in France in 1987, and was to have its premiere in the fall of 1998. The tentative title was *Madrugada* ('Dawn').

[30] 'a-shi' means 'foot' or 'reed' depending on the intonation. Takemitsu was not the first composer to grapple with this problem.

[31] *Gidayū*: a type of dramatic recitation found in *Bunraku* (traditional puppet theater).

[32] *Naniwa-bushi*: a type of narrative ballad chanted with *shamisen* accompaniment.

O: Sometimes as a listener, it is hard to follow the words in Japanese. Hikaru Hayashi[33] created an opera company called *Konnyakuza* that specializes in opera sung in Japanese, but this is a totally different art-form. It does sound strange to hear Japanese in Western operas.

T: That's right. That's why Tōru said it was really difficult to create an opera in Japanese. He could do a work like *Family Tree*[34] where there is narration, or something like *My Way of Life*[35] but that was performed in English. So he said he will do his own opera in English. He used to say, "Japanese is not suitable for songs…"

O: Yes, he really wrote very few songs and choral works.

T: The only one he worked hard on was *Wind Horse*.

O: *Handmade Proverbs* and *Grass* sound like they are very difficult to sing.

T: Those are difficult songs.

O: Were you at the premiere by the King Singers?[36]

T: They traveled to Japan for the premiere. I don't remember much about the performance. It is a very difficult work and hasn't been performed much.

---

[33] Hikaru Hayashi (1931-): Japanese composer of more than thirty operas. He is the artistic director of Opera Theater *Konnyakuza*, an opera company promoting new operas sung in Japanese.

[34] *Family Tree-Musical Verses for Young People* for narrator and orchestra (text: Shuntarō Tanikawa, 1992). It has been translated into Japanese, English, French, and Vietnamese.

[35] *My Way of Life-In Memory of Michael Vyner* for baritone, mixed chorus and orchestra (text: Ryūichi Tamura, Eng. trans. Yasunari Takahashi, 1990).

[36] Kings Singers: British a cappella ensemble which consists with six singers.

Start a new breeze

O: I want to ask you about Takemitsu's career as a producer/concert organizer. His first production was *Orchestral Space* in 1966 with Toshi Ichiyanagi.

T: That was performed only twice, and it was very difficult financially. Even I had to go out to sell tickets. They included works by Yūji Takahashi, Xenakis, and Ichiyanagi. We were happy to see a large audience in a vigorous atmosphere.

O: *Eclipse* (1966) was performed at the first concert.

T: Yes, it was at the small hall in the Nissei Theater. Seiji Ozawa happened to be at that concert, and was deeply moved by the performance of Ms. Tsuruta's *biwa* and Mr. Yokota's *shakuhachi* in *Eclipse*. It gave Tōru a hint of writing *November Steps*.

O: After *Orchestral Space* (1966, 68), he produced the contemporary music festival *Konnichi no Ongaku* ('Music Today') at the steel pavilion for the Ōsaka World Exposition in 1970.

T: After the Expo, this naturally developed into the *Music Today*[37] festival later on. But at the Expo, many people criticized him, "Why does he have to cooperate with an exposition related to the government?" Tōru didn't want to spend too much money just for one festival, but he agreed to do it because the steel pavilion was supposed to turn into a permanent facility after the Expo. In addition, artist Keiji Usami was allowed to use a laser beam, and Takemitsu did bold experiments with various speaker systems, and he was also in charge of the concert programming. Many composers came to visit from abroad, including Boulez. Baschet[38] created a unique instrument using steel. Unfortunately, after the exposition was over, nothing remained. It is such a pity.

---

[37] *Music Today*: an annual festival that lasted from 1973 to 1992. Takemitsu organized the events and introduced many different contemporary music works from Japan and abroad.

[38] The Baschet Brothers created sound sculptures and invented music instruments such as the "Cristal Baschet."

O: Even Xenakis visited the Expo. It was a great opportunity to interact with performers and composers from overseas.

T: Yes it was. After the Expo, I think Tōru thought that producing concerts was very meaningful. Mr. Seiji Tsutsumi of the Seibu Group[39] contacted him later, and discussed starting a contemporary music festival. It was when the Japanese economy was still doing well.

O: And this became the *Music Today* festival that lasted for twenty years. It was a time when Seibu Group began to prosper and the famous Kōen Street[40] and Parco Theater were built in Shibuya. The Small Theatre Jean-Jean was still there, and Shibuya was very lively back then.

T: Shibuya use to be more of a cultural center, and possessed an underlying enthusiasm, enough to create a new breeze. Thus, *Music Today* started. On the one hand, Tōru wondered whether it was appropriate for a composer to become a producer; but on the other hand, composing might have felt like self-complacency and confinement within a small cubicle for him.

O: Thanks to *Music Today*, we were able to see trends of new music around the world, and it seemed like Japan was dispatching something to the world. It also provided an opportunity for young Japanese composers.

T: Until then, we knew little about the musical trends in the world. You may notice these things if you go abroad, but if you stay in Japan, your music will not extend out into the world. Maybe it's not a composer's job to care about what kind of music is performed or what kind of performers are out there, but considering the current music situation in Japan, he thought it was necessary at that point in his career to undertake this sort of enlightening work. No matter how many pieces you compose, it means nothing if your compositions don't

---

[39] Seibu Group is a conglomerate based in Tōkyō, with interests in department stores, hotels, entertainment and railway lines.
[40] Kōen Street: one of the most popular and busiest shopping streets in Shibuya.

become a real sound. So he wanted to provide opportunities for young Japanese composers and contemporary music performers as well.

O: It is quite impressive that the festival lasted so long from 1973 until 1992, two decades all told.

T: I think that it lasted that long because of the period. Mr. Tsutsumi and the cultural manager Mr. Kinokuni supported us and overwhelmed the opposition of the bureaucracy. The Seibu Department Store is a retail company that makes money by selling products, so it must have been an enormous feat to give millions of yen to a bizarre music festival.

O: *Music Today* was criticized for receiving financial aid from a single corporation.

T: Mr. Tsutsumi and Mr. Kinokuni didn't say anything about the concert programs at all. If the concerts had been aided by the government, Tōru would have had second thoughts. He said, "If an entrepreneur says you can use the money for any good purpose, I don't mind getting help from a corporation." Back then, he was criticized for joining forces with a large corporate enterprise, but he really didn't think he was selling out. He genuinely appreciated the opportunity.

O: It was very meaningful in terms of corporate support for the Arts and its contribution to society. Had those twenty years not existed, the Japanese music scene, especially the contemporary music scene, would have been very dreary today.

T: So many composers and performers came to visit Japan including John Cage, Nexus, and Cathy Berberian.[41] There were some concerts that didn't go well, but everybody did their best.

O: Takemitsu accomplished these productions in between his spare moments from composing, so he must have been very busy.

---

[41] Cathy Berbian (1925-83): vocalist and wife of Luciano Berio. She participated in the first *Music Today* festival in 1973. Berbian invented new vocal techniques, and many composers, including John Cage and Stravinsky, composed works for her.

John Cage visited Japan in 1982.   ©Osamu Honda

T: It took more than one year to prepare each *Music Today* festival—he had to write letters to people abroad, and would have to make phone calls frequently. The whole thing seemed so chaotic and tiresome that I always told him to quit. My daughter and I also got involved; we went to pick up the guests at the airport, took them on guided tours of Kamakura, invited about twenty people over for dinner after each concert, etc. There were a lot of fun moments, but it was also tough financially, so I always asked him to quit every year. He used to complain to me when problems came up, but toward the last few years of the festival, he didn't discuss it with me anymore. He was not good at handling administrative stuff—contacting the performers, arranging for pick-up at the airport, arranging the hotel, etc. There were many tedious chores. He was always nervous when the festival neared, and he worried whether there would be enough audience members once the festival started. I was so worried about filling the seats that I thought of selling tickets on Kōen Street in Shibuya. When we had the festival at Parco Theater in Shibuya, it had a more live energy. After it moved to Ginza, it wasn't so vigorous anymore.

O: Mr. Hiroyuki conducted many new compositions.

T: Yes, Mr. Iwaki collaborated with Tōru many times together, and chamber music was his specialty. We could not have done new works without him.

O: Even now, he is an important conductor of contemporary music. Mr. Iwaki directs the Orchestra Ensemble Kanazawa, and he programs at least one contemporary piece on every concert.

T: He tries very hard to introduce new works by Japanese composers, so Mr. Iwaki's achievement should be better recognized. Even now, Ensemble Kanazawa commissions a Japanese composer once a year and premieres their work. I think it's amazing that he also educates young musicians, especially when you think about how he had overcome several tough surgeries. When I look back at *Music Today*, Mr. Iwaki, *Sound Space Arc*, and other performers worked very hard for very little money.

O: *Music Today* came to an end in 1992, and I remember Takemitsu speaking on stage at the last concert. Mr. Tsutsumi was also in the audience. I remember it was a poignant moment… I was thinking about what Tōru would do the following year.

T: I think he was relieved in a way. Twenty years means five terms in office for a prime minister or a governor, and that is way too long. You can't help for it to become a stereotyped routine. [*laughs*] But I think he was expecting and hoping for the younger generation to take over and start something new.

O: The movie director, Masahiro Shinoda said, "When I listened to Takemitsu's music long time ago, I used to think that it was fresh and new, but I can listen to it just like I do Beethoven." What do you think of the contemporary music concerts of today?

T: I went to the Composium[42] concert at the Tōkyō Opera City the other day (May 2003). The performers were totally different from those of our time. They seemed very comfortable playing contemporary music and didn't seem as if it was a big deal or anything special. The young fans formed a long line at the green room to meet the performers, and I thought Tōru's music must really sound outdated. They may even wonder, "Was this really a contemporary music?" [*laughs*]

---

[42] Composium: It is a coined word of 'composition' and 'symposium.' It is an annual music festival presented by Tōkyō Opera City.

Tape music was all done by hand. In the 1950s.

Chapter 4

Passion for Movies

The first and last segments of chapter 4 return to Takemitsu's film music. The first considers his work for various directors, including Masahiro Shinoda, Masaki Kobayashi, and Akira Kurosawa, while the final segment addresses more perfunctory but significant issues concerning the limited music budgets in Japanese films. These two portions bookend accounts on Takemitsu's love for the visual arts and on the assistants who aided Takemitsu and who sometimes notated the final autograph score, thus creating minor if understandable confusion over who actually composed the music.

'So, he loved movies…'

O'hara: Takemitsu's love for films is widely known, but when did he have time to see the movies? He must have been very busy with his work.

Takemitsu: The period during which he saw about three hundred movies a year was when he was young and lasted only a few years. In later years, he would go out for a meeting and stop by the movie theater whenever he had a spare moment. It wasn't like he was going out specifically to see the movie. If he had some spare time, he would see the movies rather than doing anything else. Or it was something like that. [*laughs*] Especially when we lived in Shibuya, he went to the movies very often.

O: I heard that after he saw a boring film, he would see another one to get rid of the bad aftertaste. [*laughs*] Did he call you and say he was going to see a movie and wouldn't need dinner or something?

T: No, he didn't call me that much. Once he left the house, I didn't know what time he would return home. [*laughs*]

O: Wow, that's not easy. [*laughs*] Didn't he tell you when he would come home?

T: When I was young, there were times when I stayed up late until he came home, but he didn't want me waiting up for him. So later, I just gave him the key and I went to sleep. If I waited for him, it was too easy for me to be sarcastic and say, "Why are you so late?" or "Where did you go?" If he said that he was coming home early to eat dinner but didn't, I couldn't really smile and be nice to him. So I pretended that I was asleep and ignored him. [*laughs*] But in later years, he stopped acting recklessly, so maybe he became boring in a way. [*laughs*]

O: Weren't you worried about his health when he did reckless things at such a young age?

T: Oh yes. Unlike other diseases, tuberculosis required years of treatment at that time. It wasn't like you get better in two or three weeks after the surgery. When he was hospitalized, he had just started out as a composer and was uncertain about his future. So when his colleagues came to visit him, he became restless and left the hospital without getting fully recovered. He started to receive more commissions for movies, performing arts, and broadcasting, but now I wonder how he survived without falling ill again. Once he escaped from the hospital and went to the broadcast station even while he was still supposed to be hospitalized.

O: At that time, movies and broadcast editing had to be done on site. Radio broadcasting first started with the government-controlled broadcasting network NHK, and the first commercial broadcasting station[1] came into being after the war. But they didn't know how to run it. Through many trials and errors, radio drama became the backbone of the station. Many young artists collaborated and experimented in ways that cannot be done today.

T: Yes, radio was still the mainstream, not TV. When I still belonged to *Geijutsu Kyōkai* ('Art Association), Naoya Uchimura went to visit U.S. and said, "America has something called commercials, and the broadcasts make money out of advertising fees." We had no idea! We all asked, "What is commercial?"

O: Takemitsu collaborated with vibrant directors and technicians such as Yasuzō Yoshimura[2] and Akira Masu[3] who utilized new techniques, such as combining the human voice and music, to create new sounds. A movie director, Masahiro Shinoda was very moved by Yoshida's

---

[1] New Japan Broadcasting Company (present day Mainichi Broadcasting System) in Ōsaka and Chūbu Nippon Broadcasting Co. in Nagoya arose in 1951 as Japan's first commercial broadcasting stations.

[2] Yasuzō Yoshimura (1921-99): Director of New Japan Broadcasting. He collaborated with Takemitsu on *Flame* ('Honō' 1955), *Sun's Testimony* ('Taiyō no Shōgen' 1958), and *Double Suicide*(1958).

[3] Akira Masu (1926-2003): acoustical engineer. He collaborated with Takemitsu on many tape works: *Flame* (1955), *Static Relief* (1955), *Euridice* (1956), *Vocalism A·I* (1956), *Tree-Sky-Bird* (1956).

radio drama *Double Suicide* ('Shinjū Ten no Amijima' 1958) and, eleven years later, he made his own movie version with *Double Suicide* (1969).

T: It was a period when they could put time and money into radio drama. When Tōru was making *Flame* ('Honō' 1955) at the New Japan Broadcast Station, he was stuck in the studio and worked all night long for one or two months straight. Back then, they cut the recording tape and spliced it together by hand for editing. He didn't come home at all, and it wasn't easy for me either.

O: One wonderful drama was that of *Yaoya Oshichi*,[4] performed by Kyōko Kishida.[5] Takemitsu edited the tape of *Flame* and transformed it into *Static Relief* (1955); later it became *Vocalism A·I* (1956) using the voices of Kyōko Kishida and Hiroshi Mizushima.

T: Similar to *Flame*, *Mask* (1959/60) was a radio drama based on Fumiko Enchi's novel *Women's mask* ('Onna Men' 1959). Even though it was only the background music, Tōru didn't dash it off, but he had also experimented with it a lot, as if it were an independent piece.

O: It seems that he didn't intentionally try to experiment, but rather he had put all his energy and effort into it, and as a result he tested different ideas through trials and errors until he turned it into a decent piece. But again, it was that kind of time period back then.

T: There was a radio drama with Mr. Tanikawa, *Death of a Man- Billy the Kid*. I look back at that period—and I am not exaggerating—I think that the passion for radio broadcasting was pretty amazing.

O: Movies are printed in film, so there is a possibility to have re-runs, but I hope that there will be many opportunities to examine the greatness of those radio dramas and other TV programs. I am sure they have the potential to move the audience of today.

T: I wonder if the recordings still exist.

----

[4] *Yaoya Oshichi*: a traditional play based on a true story in the Edo period ca. 1670.
[5] Kyōko Kishida (1930-): Japanese actress. Kishida collaborated on Takemitsu's tape works *Vocalism A·I* (1956), *Tree-Sky-Birds* (1956), and the radio drama *Death of a Man* (1957).

O: Recordings of the TV drama and documentary films rarely survive, as it was a time before video tape came into use. But fortunately we did find many recordings of the radio dramas.

T: I would like to listen to these again.

O: I can imagine it was difficult to have Takemitsu working and staying overnight in the recording studio. Did you visit him in the studio?

T: Every so often, I did go there to bring a change of clothes and a lunch box for him. But we lived in Kamakura back then, and it was not easy to get to the studio. Probably that's why Tōru just stayed in the studio rather than come all the way home to Kamakura. Even when he started to work on *Kwaidan* (1965), directed by Masaki Kobayashi, he hardly came home. Not only was he composing film music, but also he was working on sound effects, such as squeaking doors and blizzards sounds. After they recorded the original source sounds, they would do the final mix in the studio. It was all done by hand, so they spent days and nights at the studio. Back then, they spent a lot of time on a single movie, as was the case in *Kwaidan* or *Woman in the Dunes* (1964).

O: Was Takemitsu's health better by that time?

T: His health was much better when he was doing *Kwaidan* and *Woman in the Dunes*, and the doctor said, "I can't believe you recovered without having surgery." It wasn't just a shadow or a mere perforation he had in in his llungs; he had holes in both of his lungs that were the size of a chicken egg. I heard that when one has a big hole like that in one lung, it is very difficult to cure it.

T: And that hole shrank?

O: The focus calcified, and the hole became smaller and smaller. But as there was no complete cure for tuberculosis back then, the doctor was always warning him that it could return if he weren't careful. I always had that in mind, so I might have nagged him too much.

T: In his old photos, I see him with cigarettes, but wasn't that bad for his health...?

O: When he was young, he was a big-time heavy smoker. When I cleaned his room, the ashtray near the piano was piled up with full of cigarette ash and the ashtray was all yellow. His doctor said, "Your respiratory system has a problem, so you can drink a little, but you'd better quit smoking." But Tōru said, "I need this to compose," and continued to smoke. But when Maki was about in first grade, he declared on my birthday, "I don't have anything to buy for you, so I will quit smoking from today." But there was no way he could give up smoking! At least he tried not to smoke in front of me. If he went outside to smoke behind my back, that was fine by me. Still, I would often say to our friends in front of him on purpose, "Tōru-san quit smoking on my birthday." I figured that would make him smoke less. [*laughs*]

O: I see—so he could not quit smoking that easily. By the way, did Takemitsu conceive ideas for concert pieces by experimenting with them in film music?

T: I don't think he intentionally did it that way. There were times when he found something effective in a movie and later used it in a concert piece, or vice versa. For him, I don't think there were any distinctions between concert music and film music.

O: In the U.S., it seems that the dividing line between film music composers and concert music composers is strong. But this wasn't the case with Takemitsu.

T: No, he did not make such a line between them. Some composers in the past thought of film music as a part-time job, but not Tōru.

O: He really liked movies. For that reason, I have the impression of Takemitsu being a man with 'eyes' as well as a man with 'ears.' Do you feel that way, too?

T: You may be right.

Art and Music

O: When he was young, Takemitsu wrote a critical essay on Paul Klee[6] in an art journal. I heard that he was introduced to the publisher by Shūzō Takiguchi.

T: I think it was through art that Tōru and Mr. Takiguchi became so close. Tōru was extremely interested in art and made friends with painters and artists very easily. And he was more passionate about going to art exhibitions than going to music concerts.

O: I didn't know he went to art exhibitions that often.

T: Even in later years, when he went abroad, the first thing he would do was to go to the art exhibitions. He went quite frequently. When he was young, he couldn't decide whether he wanted to be a composer, or a mystery writer, or an art critic. [*laughs*]

O: I knew that he went to the movies when he travelled abroad, but I didn't know he went to art museums that often.

T: He didn't like to go to traditional art museums to see the so-called masterpieces, but he liked new art—modern art exhibitions. We had totally different tastes. I was interested in history, so I liked to go to traditional museums. We always quarreled over it. [*laughs*]

O: Wasn't it the same with his taste in literature?

T: Yes, yes. Rather than the masterpieces, he liked surrealism and such.

O: And among his old friends were modern artists and authors.

T: During the *Jikken Kōbō* days, there were Tetsurō Komai, Katsuhiro Yamaguchi, Shōzō Kitadai, and Mitsuo Kanō. Hisao Dōmoto went to

---

6 "Paul Klee and Music," *Atelier*, June 1951.

France and became close to Takemitsu after he returned to Japan. As for foreign artists, Tōru was close to Jasper Johns[7] and Sam Francis.[8]

O: What about Keiji Usami?[9]

T: Before working together at the Expo '70,[10] both Mr. Usami and Tōru were invited to the U.S. by the Rockefeller Foundation and they met in New York. Tōru said that he was always inspired by Mr. Usami.

O: At that time, the U.S. was a leader in the fields of modern art and music, and art galleries played a prominent role in the modern art world. It was a time when Sōgetsu Kaikan Hall held various events that combined modern and avant-garde art with music.

T: It was the time of Sōfū Teshigahara.[11] There were various events.

O: Where did Takemitsu meet Jasper Johns?

T: Our first trip abroad was to Hawaii. Even before going to New York for the premiere of *November Steps* in 1967, we had visited Hawaii in 1964. We met Jasper at that time. Tōru was invited to an event organized by the East-West Center at the University of Hawaii, and so we stayed in Hawaii for about two months. Since Maki was about three years old, I stayed in Hawaii with her while Tōru went on to the mainland. In San Francisco, Tōru attended David Tudor's concert and met John Cage and Jasper Johns there. John Cage was also invited to Hawaii and the three of them came back to Hawaii together. They all traveled around Hawaii and became good buddies.

---

[7] Jasper Johns (1930-): American painter. Johns met Takemitsu in San Francisco in 1964. Takemitsu consulted Johns about the English title of *November Steps*.

[8] Sam Francis (1923-94): American painter. Takemitsu dedicated *Cross Talk* (1968) to Francis.

[9] Keiji Usami(1940-): Japanese artist. Usami designed the covers for all of Takemitsu's essay books.

[10] Expo '70: World Fair in Ōsaka, 1970. Takemitsu and Usami were the producers at the Steel Pavilion.

[11] Sōfū Teshigahara (1900-79): founder of Sōgetsu School of Ikebana flower arrangement. He founded Sōgetsu Art Center in 1958 and provided a space for avant-garde art. His son, Hiroshi is the movie director of *Woman in the Dunes*.

O: After that, Johns came to Japan, correct?

T: Yes, Jasper came with us when we went back to Japan. He had an exhibition at the Minami Gallery. Minami Gallery exhibited young avant-garde artists such as Mitsuo Kanō and Keiji Usami. Tōru would go to the galleries more often than to concerts, and he went out to eat and drink with the artists he met there. He really liked art.

O: He was no doubt stimulated by many things in art.

T: I think so. He interacted more often with artists than with musicians.

O: I've often thought that Takemitsu's brain was able to convert the stimuli from his eye directly into a sound without changing it to something abstract first. It seems to me that if he were to see a movie alone in a dark theater in some unknown language, he would be the only one who could conceive of sound and music to go along with it. Likewise, I think that when he saw a painting, he might have heard its rhythm and sound.

T: If he had the talent, he would have become a painter. That's how much he loved art.

O: I imagined that if Takemitsu was a painter, he might have been like Kandinsky and Klee whose canvases are rhythmic and musical. I wonder if images and sound were going back and forth inside Takemitsu's brain.

T: Again, there was that Miró exhibition at Musée d'art Mercian in Karuizawa. I myself find Miró's painting to be really musical. So Tōru must have been inspired by seeing these kinds of paintings.

O: I think movies and art were something he could not separate from music. When he was in the hospital, Takemitsu adorned many recipes with illustrations drawn with color pencils.[12] They are beautifully drawn, just like his music scores.

---

[12] Takemitsu wrote fifty-one recipes of his own with detailed cooking instructions. It was published after his death as *Silent Garden*, Tōkyō Shinchōsha (1999).

T: His doctor said that it was amazing to be able to write down recipes during chemotherapy. I don't think the illustrations were especially skillful, but they were drawn meticulously, like those of an elementary school child. [*laughs*]

O: On the hospital bed, abstract artist Tatsuoki Nanbata left a series of works drawn with ballpoint pens of many colors including red, green, pink, and blue. This was in the last years of his own life, and I feel there is a connection between these drawings and Takemitsu's. The drawings in Takemitsu's recipe book were not like those of a child, but it was drawn with his whole heart. I could even hear music in them, too.

T: Oh really, from Mr. Nanbata's pictures? Tōru liked his son Fumio's paintings too.

Takemitsu's assistants

O: I heard that several assistants came to help Takemitsu to write parts and copy full scores in order to meet deadlines for his film commissions. I interviewed one of his assistants, Shinichirō Ikebe,[13] about his experience. He became Takemitsu's assistant when he was still a student at Tōkyō National University of Fine Arts and Music (currently Tōkyō University of the Arts). He was very surprised to see that Takemitsu composed as if it were no big deal.[14] I heard that he went to Takemitsu's house in the morning, ate lunch with him, and would sometimes work over night.

---

[13] Shinichirō Ikebe (1943-): renowned Japanese composer. He became Takemitsu's film music assistant in the 1970s, and collaborating with Takemitsu on *Under the Blossoming Cherry Tree* ('Sakura no Mori no Mankai no Shita' 1975).

[14] When interviewed for the *Complete Takemitsu Edition*, Ikebe said, "In my 'territory' where I studied music, I was told to set my mind firmly, prepare special things carefully, and compose as if it were some sort of a ceremony. Actually it should not be a big deal like that."

T: Yes, many people came to assist Tōru. When we lived in Kamakura, Masanobu Higure was the assistant. They worked for director Noboru Nakamura, and also worked on Susumu Hani's *Bad Boys* ('Furyō Shōnen' 1961). After we moved to Meguro in Tōkyō, his assistant was Kurōdo Mōri,[15] and then Motohiko Adachi and Manabu Kawai. And then, his last assistant was Shinichirō Ikebe.

O: Was Mr. Ikebe the longest?

T: No, Mr. Ikebe wasn't the longest. I think Mr. Mōri was the longest. He helped Tōru for a long time, until his last days.

O: When did Mr. Mōri pass away?

T: I don't remember how old he was when he died. We received a phone call saying that he had a cancer. He said, "I am only forty five years old. I don't want to die yet." I didn't know what to say. He died two or three years after that. We felt so sorry for him. After that, Norio Fukushi came to help Tōru once, and Yoshio Hachimura came to make a fair copy of his full scores once or twice.

O: Mr. Hachimura himself left many good pieces.

T: I agree. Tōru was very impressed with Mr. Hachimura's talent. When Mr. Hachimura was hospitalized, Mr. Mōri was right beside him, taking care of him the whole time. I think Mr. Mōri was present at his death. And about ten years later, it was Mr. Mōri... After Mr. Mōri died, Yui Kakinuma came to help Tōru. With film music, Tōru needed to complete a huge amount of work in a limited time. His assistant would wait in an adjacent room to make a fair copy of his score, so Tōru drove himself into a corner. I really miss Mr. Mōri and Mr. Hachimura. When I look back, many young and talented people came to support Tōru, so he was able to continue his work despite his weak health. My job was to prepare meals for his assistants when they stayed over. It

---

15 Kurōdo Mōri (1950-97): Japanese composer. Mōri collaborated with Takemitsu on *Antonio Gaudi* (1984), and conducted Takemitsu's score for in *Rikyū* (1989), *Dream/Window* (1992).

was very busy time but I also had a chance to chat with them. These are all cherished memories.

O: When I researched the film scores at the Documentation Centre of Modern Japanese Music, I found many manuscripts that say 'K. MORI.'

T: The staff paper belonged to Mr. Mōri. Tōru used staff paper with Mr. Mōri's signature without any hesitation. 'MORI' is written right at the bottom of the staves. Tōru didn't really care about those things, and I asked him, "Why don't you make your own music paper?" and he said, "Nah, I don't need it." Mr. Mōri brought his own staff paper when he came to help Tōru with film scores. The problem was Tōru used this staff paper not only for his film scores, but also for his concert music. The other day, Meirin Takeda[16] said, "Is this film music Takemitsu's? Isn't it actually Mōri's?" I didn't know why he asked that kind of a question, but then I saw the printed name in the manuscript.

O: I found a manuscript with Shinichirō Ikebe's name on it. [*laughs*]

T: Even the manuscript for his last guitar piece *In the Woods* (1995)— and this was a solo piece and no one else made a fair copy of, so Tōru definitely wrote it by himself—even that manuscript has the name 'MORI' on it. [*laughs*]

O: If Asaka-san doesn't clarify this problem about the signatures on the manuscripts, maybe some pieces will not be considered Takemitsu's original compositions in ages to come? [*laughs*]

T: That's true! But what can I do? [*laughs*]

O: When Takemitsu wrote the final copy, it is easy to see this from the handwriting, but it is confusing when someone else wrote it. That's why there are some scores that are believed to be Takemitsu's handwritten manuscripts, but still have other people's handwriting on them too. Can you tell that it's his handwriting just by looking at the letters or notations?

---

[16] Meirin Takeda (1937-2003): musicologist, music critic.

T: Yes, I can. In some cases, Tōru notated the score but asked me to write things such as the title or the text. I can tell my own writing of course.

O: So sometimes the music was notated by Takemitsu, while the words were written by Asaka-san.

T: Yes, that is true.

O: Now I see why it's confusing. Your handwriting is similar to Takemitsu.

T: Everyone says that—Tōru and I didn't think so.

O: Did you ever write the music notation, too?

T: I wrote some part of the score of *Requiem for Strings* but nothing else. There were no copy machines back then, so I wrote some of the individual parts. But our handwriting was similar, so many people got confused.

O: It is like Bach. The handwritten music notation and letters of J.S. Bach's wife, Anne Magdelena, were written very similar to her husband's, and even Bach scholars cannot always tell the difference between the two. [*laughs*] So please be sure to inform us which scores are Tōru's own handwriting. In any case, he should've made his own staff paper.

T: Writers make their own manuscript paper. Tōru didn't bother to think about how important this would be after he died. After composing and becoming published by Schott Japan, he thought he didn't need to keep his own handwritten copies. He threw away the manuscripts of some of his film scores.

O: Oh, no. What a pity. [*laughs*]

His Favorite movies

O: Have you seen all the movies in which Takemitsu was involved?

T: Tōru always brought me to the preview so I saw most of them. The only three movies I couldn't see—*Fulfilled Life* ('Mitasareta Seikatsu' 1962) directed by Susumu Hani, *With Beauty and Sorrow* ('Utsukushisa to Kanashimi to' 1965) and *Clouds at Sunset* ('Akanegumo' 1967) directed by Mr. Shinoda—were when Maki was little and when I was hospitalized.

O: In the *Complete Takemitsu Edition*, we counted ninety-six film scores. Among the movies that he was involved in, do you know which one was his favorite?

T: His favorite... He didn't say much about it. It is different when you say you like the movie itself, or when you get involved and say that it went well. I think the one he thought went well is *Woman in the Dunes* (1964).

O: *Woman in the Dunes* is shown in foreign countries often.

T: When *Woman in the Dunes* was shown in England, several older women left their seats in the middle of the movie as if they were saying, "What kind of movie is this?" They were like the PTA mothers and kicked their seats and left.

O: It must have been the movie and not the music. [*laughs*]

T: I guess so. I don't think the movie is that extreme. But on the other hand, at a film music festival in Switzerland,[17] where Tōru was the invited composer, they showed the same movie and an older woman who was the usher told me, "I was so moved. It was wonderful! I am so happy to see such a great movie today." Since I saw that in London where some people left the theater, Maki and I were so surprised. *Woman in the Dunes* and Mr. Teshigahara's other film *The Pitfall*

---

[17] CineMusic Festival was held in Gstaad Switzerland in March 1995.

('Otoshiana' 1962) are wonderful movies even when we see them today. The theme of *The Pitfall* is about unions, so I thought it might feel dated, but it hasn't at all.

O: The cinematography is good. The actors are good too. Hisashi Ikawa is especially good. And the music is excellent.

T: That score was a joint work with Toshi Ichiyanagi and Yūji Takahashi, both of whom played the prepared piano. It was very effective. That period of Mr. Teshigahara's was superb.

O: I heard that Ichiyanagi and Takahashi improvised on the piano while watching part of the movie on the big screen in front of them. They not only played the keyboard but also hit the strings, inserted an eraser between the strings, and made various sounds. It was effective that the recording was done with improvisation. In that movie, Takemitsu appears in one scene as a passenger on a bus. Do you have any comment on that?

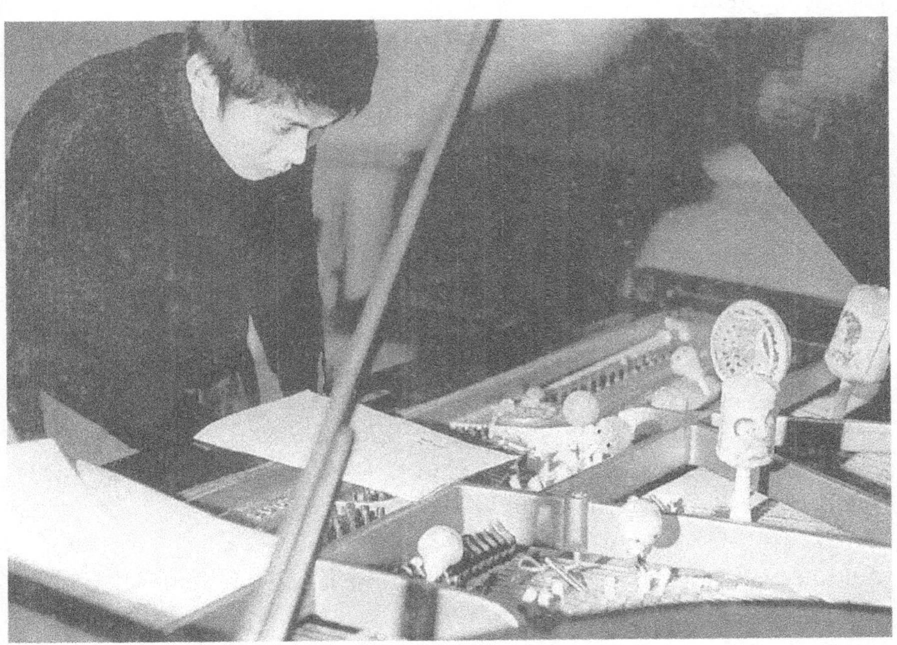

Yuji Takahashi playing prepared piano for *The Pitfall* in 1962.

T: I don't know why he appeared in a movie. I have no comment. [*laughs*]

O: Do you have any other memorable movies?

T: Let me think… Tōru and I have left such an indelible impression on *Double Suicide* (1969). I also like *The Assassin* ('Ansatsu' 1964) by Mr. Shinoda, *Harakiri* ('Seppuku' 1962) and *Kwaidan* (1965) by Mr. Kobayashi. There were many incidents with *Ran* directed by Mr. Kurosawa.

A Major Fight with a Famed Director

O: I heard that there was a difference of opinion between the director Kurosawa and Takemitsu…

T: I clearly remember when Tōru took me to a preview of *Dodes'kaden* (1970). It was held at the Tōhō film studio in a staff-members only room called 'Number One.' Tōru was so anxious about the result because that was the first time Tōru collaborated with Mr. Kurosawa. Tōru asked me so many times to go together to 'Number One.' I was kind of scared of Mr. Kurosawa and didn't want to be the only wife in the staff-only preview room, so I said to him, "I don't want to go. But I will definitely see it at the theater." Then Tōru got so mad and we had a fight. So, reluctantly, I went to see it with him. Probably the younger people nowadays would be OK with it, but my generation was uncomfortable to go to such a place. But Tōru didn't care much about it. And when the movie was over and the lights turned on, Mr. Kurosawa was very cheerful and said, "Takemitsu-kun, thank you." and shook his hand. I wanted to hide and leave immediately, but Tōru introduced me, "This is my wife." Mr. Kurosawa smiled and said, "Thank you very much!" I was so relieved and kind of felt deflated. I couldn't possibly imagine that they would have a big fight over *Ran* in years to come.

O: *Dodes'kaden* has a different flavor compared with other Kurosawa movies. It is an omnibus film (a film with multiple stories) and music connects one story to the next.

T: Yes, it is not the usual Kurosawa movie with a bold grand scheme.

O: And there was a gap until *Ran*.

T: After *Dodes'kaden*, they got along pretty well, and Tōru visited Mr. Kurosawa's house many times. The plan was eventually cancelled, but he was consulted on the joint Japan-U.S. movie *Tora, Tora, Tora!*[18]

O: And later on they would work together in *Ran*.

T: Tōru was very into *Ran*, and had various ideas for the musical structure of *Ran* such as making a collage from narration and singing in Japanese *kabuki* and *gidayū*. Mr. Kurosawa said that was very interesting and agreed to the idea, but after the movie started rolling, Mr. Kurosawa could only hear Mahler's music...He could not accept anything else. He asked Tōru to write music like Mahler, and Tōru said, "Then why don't you use Mahler's music?"

O: Movie and music—each with their own strong character—collide with one another and cannot be reconciled. I read the interview by Teruyo Nogami and Ichirō Uno, who were Kurosawa and Takemitsu's managers respectively.

T: Once it is finished, a movie is the director's possession, but Tōru was criticized for many things after the recording was already done. Tōru had confidence in his own music, so I guess he wanted to express his opinion.

O: I heard that Kurosawa slid several letters under the door to Takemitsu's hotel room. Does any such letter still exist?

---

[18] *Tora, Tora, Tora!* (1970): the film has been originally planned to be directed by Francis Coppola and Kurosawa.

T: I saw one back then, and I found a copy of their correspondence after Tōru died. According to Mr. Kurosawa's letter, probably Takemitsu's music was totally different from what he expected. There were very detailed requests with regards to his music. And there were things that might make a composer upset. And then I read the letter that Tōru wrote to Mr. Kurosawa: "You can chop up my music however you want, and use it as you wish. It would be better to ask somebody else to compose and redo it again, but we already recorded with the Sapporo Symphony Orchestra with Mr. Iwaki as the conductor and used a lot of money. So you can cut and paste however you want it, but please take out my name from the title and everything."

O: That was sent to Kurosawa?

T: I guess so. Two of them are already gone, so we won't publish it, but when I read it back then, I was moved by their earnest attitudes.

O: I wonder how it would've been to hear Takemitsu's original plan of using a collage of *gidayū* and *kabuki* narration. It would have been interesting to hear it.

T: I think so too. But when I look at *Ran* now, the music actually works very well. [*laughs*]

O: Yes, the staff must have had a hard time though. [*laughs*]

T: Abroad, the music of *Ran* has a good reputation. In L.A., Tōru received the Los Angeles Film Critics Awards. I don't know what Mr. Kurosawa thought about it though. My guess is Tōru didn't actually get along well with Mr. Kurosawa. He used to say, "Fumio Hayasaka and Masaru Satō are better composers for Mr. Kurosawa's movies."

O: Hayasaka was in charge for *Drunken Angel* ('Yoidore Tenshi' 1948), *Rashōmon* (1950), and *The Seven Samurai* (1954). Satō did *Yōjimbō* (1961), *High and Low* ('Tengoku to Jigoku' 1963), and *Red Beard* ('Akahige' 1965). There are many calculated cuts during this period, so I think the type of music was already playing in Kurosawa's mind.

T: That is right. A Kurosawa movie has its own rhythm, sometimes that of Bizet's *The Girl of Arles* and sometimes of Ravel's *Bolero*. He edits the movie with that rhythm, so the music needs to fit in with his idea…

O: There was a movie called *Night on Earth* (1991) by Jim Jarmusch,[19] and Takemitsu's music was finished but it was not used.

T: There is a film union in the U.S., and it is difficult to hire people who are not in the union members. There must have been a contract problem or something, but I don't know exactly why it was not used. But I think at the end, the director Jarmusch did not get the music that he wanted. Maybe when he commissioned Tōru, he had a sound in mind like that of *Woman in the Dunes* or *Kwaidan*. *Night* is a movie with a series of episodes that occur simultaneously in different countries on earth. Tōru's idea was to create the same music varying the editing and instrumentation according to each country.

O: I heard that one reason might be that movie itself would have been weaker than the music…

T: I don't think so, but Tōru thought the composition went very well, so he felt disappointed.

O: At the end, a different composer would compose for the movie, but I listened to the phantom piece by Takemitsu and it was very beautiful.

T: Tōru thought his idea was executed well and liked it very much. So it was really a pity. But even after that, Jarmusch and Tōru used to go out for a drink, and they seemed to have no ill feeling and still kept their respect for each other.

O: I heard that he visited Jarmusch's house in New York.

T: Jarmusch lived in Soho in New York, and I also visited him together with Tōru. His apartment building looked a hundred or two hundred years old, but inside was a large studio with beautiful

---

[19] Jim Jarmusch (1953-): American movie director specializes in independent films.

hardwood floors, and no furniture. There was not a single chair, so we sat on the floor. He had many CDs, and he owned many copies of Tōru's music, which enabled them to get along well. So that's why, when he got this commission, Tōru was very happy and did his best. But later, he used part of the film score for *Family Tree* (1992), so I think it turned out fine.

O: There are many types of film directors, so film music composers must have a hard time. But I heard that the director Nagisa Ōshima left everything up to Takemitsu once he commissioned him.

T: Mr. Ōshima said, "Takemitsu composed beautiful scores for Shinoda's and Onchi's films, but the music for my *The Ceremony* ('Gishiki' 1971) is not. Why only mine..."

O: That's why Takemitsu's next Ōshima work, *Dear Summer Sister* ('Natsu no Imōto' 1972), has beautiful music. [*laughs*] Unlike the old method of watching the screen and dubbing the music at the same time, this music score was recorded separately from the scene, carefully timing the minutes and seconds. And then they dubbed it onto the sound track later. So as for the director, he didn't know how it would sound until the end of the production?

T: I think so.

O: I heard that Takemitsu was close to the director Hideo Onchi,[20] who produced *Longing* ('Akogare' 1966) and *The Encounter* ('Meguriai' 1968).

T: Mr. Onchi was blamed for actually killing a cow in *The Female Body* ('Nyotai' 1964), and Tōru wrote him a letter of encouragement.[21] After that, they became good friends—so there are many movies with Mr. Onchi.

---

[20] Hideo Onichi (1933-): movie director. Takemitsu composed music for seven films, including *The Izu Dancer* ('Izu no Odoriko' 1967).

[21] Takemitsu wrote an essay addressed to Onchi in the film journal *Eiga Geijutsu* (Nov. 1965). "The wound that was torn down in *Woman's Body* is deeper than the murdered cow."

O: Mr. Onchi's movies always have a human element and warmth in his works.

T: The most recent film, *Warabi no kou* (2003), is the same way.

O: Among all the music for the Kobayashi's movies, the film score for *Glowing Autumn* ('Moeru Aki' 1978) is different.

T: Even the movie itself is different from the usual Kobayashi film, and it is unlike Mr. Kobayashi... It is different from *Kwaidan* or *Harakiri*.

O: The other day, I found this film score and Takemitsu's hand written roll chart. It is a chart that details the number of minutes and seconds for each scene, and at the end, he wrote, "Will it end up being a big failure?" Do you know about this?

T: Really? I didn't know that. But I remember he was struggling with this one. It is different from other Kobayashi films. Hiroyuki Itsuki put the lyrics to the music and turned the main theme into a song. It wound up different from the original plan, and Tōru thought it might not fit the movie.

O: I was impressed that even Takemitsu was afraid that it might flop. By the way, this song became a single. The group Hi-Fi Set produced it and became a hit.

T: I receive hardly any royalties for Takemitsu's music, but *Glowing Autumn* earns the most. [*laughs*]

Passion for Movies

O: Movies have big budgets, but it is not that easy: you cannot re-record the music just because it didn't come out well.

T: Especially in film music, you cannot spend a lot of money recording and then cancel it for economical reasons. So the trust between the director and the composer is very important. Once you ask a composer to write, it is hard to redo any of the recording sessions.

O: That's why they need faith in each other.

T: That's right.

O: Takemitsu's passion for film music was really amazing. I felt this very strongly after editing the *Complete Takemitsu Edition*.

T: Mr. Hayasaka, Mr. Mayuzumi, and Mr. Akutagawa opened the path of film music, but it wasn't taken seriously for a long time. In movies, music is placed last in terms of time and money. If shooting gets delayed, then the finishing date is delayed, then the editing is delayed—yet the release date is already fixed. This influences how the music is done. Sometimes the weather didn't cooperate, or the actors' schedules didn't work out and then the film would be delayed and delayed. It was nice if they had ten or more days to finish the music sound track, but since completion dates could not be changed, the time for the music was sometimes compressed. Also budget wise, since they used money for everything else first, and the music would only get the leftover. Compared to foreign films, Japanese films budget unbelievably small amounts of money for music. It is very expensive to rent a studio for a whole day, so the recording sessions get reduced from three days to one day, and the numbers of performers goes down, good musicians are too expensive to hire...

O: Takemitsu continued on in that kind of environment.

T: He was young, eager to do it, and above all, he loved movies, so he wanted to change the system. He said, "If the music is good, the movie will be better."

O: If there is a big budget, the composer can write for a large ensemble, can get enough time for recording, and write in a grand scale. Sometimes, music can help to elevate the movie.

T: For example, the instrumentation for *The Assassin*'s music was only *shakuhachi* and prepared piano despite having a larger budget, but viewers would never think that they used only two instruments because they didn't have time and money. They wouldn't ask, "Why is there only one guitar in this scene?" In order to allow for a bigger ensemble, Tōru would say, "You can reduce my composing fee, so please gather good performers." But it wouldn't change the situation even if he did that. So he used to say, "They might not accept it, but we need to insist on raising the budget for film music. We have to say out loud that we are trying our very best, so we will not compose music if the budget is lower than this amount. This is not simply my problem, but we must also raise the status of film music in Japan. We should not just obey as we are told. We need to change it on the spot." Tōru's film music manager Mr. Uno understood the predicaments of the movie companies, so I imagine he had a hard time mediating between them.

O: At a press conference for *Rising Sun* (1993)[22] by director Philip Kaufman, Takemitsu said he wanted to emphasize that, "The budget and time spent in Japanese film music is too little."

T: I think he maintained his passion toward movies until he died. He was so fortunate to be able to work on what he loved, and to collaborate with wonderful directors at a time when they were able to make a movie with time and care.

---

[22] *Rising Sun* was Takemitsu's first and only film produced abroad.

At a movie theater in Nagano. 1973.

Chapter 5

Daily life of a composer

Chapter 5 takes place at the Takemitsu cottage in Miyota, a village west of Tōkyō in the Japanese Alps. The couple purchased this cottage in the mid-1960s and, owing to its quiet setting and natural environs, it became Tōru's preferred location for composing. Also included here is a necessarily sketchy but still fascinating look at Takemitsu's compositional process. Besides Takemitsu's professionalism and his hearty work ethic, the interview reveals the central importance of visual, literary, and conceptual ideas to the nature of each individual work. Chapter 5 concludes with a personal account of his illness and his final days in the hospital, including his chance listening to a recording of the complete *St. Matthew Passion*, a work that held great personal significance for Takemitsu—and for Asaka-san—as the interview makes abundantly clear.

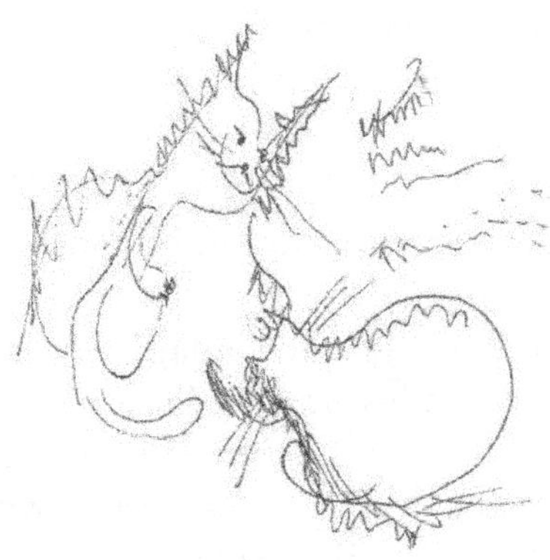

MI.YO.TA

O'hara: When did you first come to the town of Miyota in Nagano prefecture?

Takemitsu: The very first time we came to Miyota was when Maki was still in kindergarten. It was before we went to New York for the world premiere of *November Steps*.

O: *November Steps* was written in 1967.

T: At that time, we were renting a small house in Seijō in Tōkyō. When Tōru won a fellowship grant from the Rockefeller Foundation to live in the U.S. for one year, we asked if the grant could coincide with the time of the *November Steps* premiere. Since we didn't want to waste a year's rent in Seijō, we left all our belongings in Miyota and then took off to the U.S. So I guess we came here two years before that. By the time when Maki entered kindergarten, we were already here.

O: It has been forty years already.

T: Last year, there was a fortieth year anniversary celebration for this Fugen mountain villa. We came to this town two years after the establishment of the villa, so that's right, it has been forty years. Until then, we were living in a rented house in Tōkyō, so it felt like this was our first home. Tōru wanted to come to Miyota as often as he could, but he had other obligations, so he tried to stay here between May and October to focus on composing. *November Steps* was composed here.

O: I see, *November Steps* was written here in Miyota.

T: Tōru really liked the nature and the climate here, so I think he was able to concentrate entirely on his own work. Orchestra pieces and other large pieces were mainly written here, but plays, films, and television works were written in Tōkyō since there were meetings and he needed to see the daily rushes. But when he was composing concert pieces, he turned down other offers and came to Miyota as often as he could to focus on composing. He couldn't do two things at the same time.

O: Was he in his late thirties?

T: Yes. He was about thirty-seven.

O: So from that point on his masterpieces were mainly written here.

T: That is right. He composed a lot of his works here.

O: There is a song called *MI.YO.TA*[1] by Takemitsu to a poem of Shuntarō Tanikawa. Whenever I come here, I can't help but recall the imagery of the song. One line goes: "Sunlight pouring through the trees, a silhouette approaching; far beyond, a blue sky appears…"

T: These are very sensitive lines from Mr. Tanikawa. I wonder how Tōru would feel. He liked Asama Mountain, larch trees, and 'tree' in general. He composed a piece called *Music of Trees* (1961) and our daughter was born in the same year, so we named her *Ma-Ki* ('real tree'). This area is now full of houses that go all the way to the top of the mountain, but back then it was just a rural countryside. There was nothing when we came here, just woods and fields. We were able to see Asama Mountain very clearly. But when I say he liked mountains and trees, people would think he was a nature-oriented person, but he also enjoyed the city life, too. He actually liked the hustle and bustle, and the neon-lit streets.

O: Well, he liked movies, so no wonder. Movie theaters are located in densely populated areas.

T: Yes, that's right. After he had completed a piece, he often looked forward to going out for a drink with his friends in Tōkyō. He didn't have any problem with the city life, but I guess it was more suitable to compose here.

---

[1] Takemitsu composed this tune in his twenties when he was Mayuzumi's assistant. Mayuzumi remembered this melody, and sang it in Takemitsu's funeral.

From left: Kazuko Enomoto (painter), Maki, Shuntarō Tanikawa, Hideko Fukushima, Asaka, and Tōru.

O: Among Takemitsu's works, many have titles that are related to nature such as tree, star, and birds.[2] It seems, perhaps, as if his works have something in common with the serene and tranquil atmosphere here in Miyota. Were those works mostly written here?

T: Yes, after we bought this house, they were. But back then, it was severely cold in the depths of winter and we didn't have a good heating system like today, so it was impossible for us to stay here during the whole winter. After we moved from Shibuya to the house near Tama Lake in Higashi-Murayama, he liked that environment too, so there are some pieces that were written there.[3]

O: How did Takemitsu spend his time here?

T: I wasn't with him that often. After Maki entered elementary school, Tōru would come here by himself, and I visited about once a week. After Maki became independent and left the house, Tōru and I lived together under one roof.

O: When he was young, he used to come here alone?

T: There were many times when he came alone. When my daughter was on her summer break, we all stayed here together. Otherwise, he came here by himself.

Daily Routine of Takemitsu

O: I think many readers are curious to know the daily life of Takemitsu—how his day started, and how he composed here in Miyota or in Tōkyō. So I would like to step in further and ask some detailed information. [*laughs*] What time did he usually wake up?

---

[2] For instance *A Flock Descends into the Pentagonal Garden* (1977), *Rain Tree* (1981), *Wind Horse* for mixed chorus (1961/66).

[3] *Waterways* (1977-78) was inspired by Lake Tama.

T: Most mornings, he woke rather early. Many say that people with low blood pressure cannot wake up early but he could. His blood pressure was very low; his high was in the nineties and low was in the sixties. I liked to sleep in, so I always wished he would wake up later. Even when he came home at 2 AM, he would wake up at seven or eight in the morning. And then he would shake me, "Now wake up! Wake up!" [*laughs*]

O: He is like a wheedling child. [*laughs*]

T: I used to wonder how he can survive with so little sleep. And he always took a bath in the morning.

O: Did he prefer rice or bread for breakfast?

T: He liked rice when he was young, but in his late life he preferred bread.

O: Was it white bread or baguette?

T: Sometimes it was white bread; sometimes it was croissant, or baguette. When the bread became stale, I made French toast. Anyway, he had a big breakfast.

O: Did he drink coffee or tea?

T: Coffee, and then always yogurt.

O: Which brand of yogurt?

T: Ever since the old days, he would only eat *Meiji*'s Bulgaria yogurt. I put all kinds of fruits in it. And I added another dish with some protein like ham, sausage or bacon. It was a big breakfast.

O: Wow, it's like at a hotel. [*laughs*]

T: And salad, so the morning time was very busy for me. But he wouldn't eat fresh vegetables saying, "I am not a rabbit." [*laughs*] So I prepared cooked vegetable salads such as potatoes, green beans, and broccoli.

O: Takemitsu kept you very busy on top of waking you up early in the morning.

T: Yes, I hear that for many self-employed people, the day and night are reversed, but Tōru's morning started early. But, it was not a rushed morning, rather slow and relaxed. We chatted a lot, so it might have been the most fun part of the day.

O: So he woke up regularly at eight in the morning. Did he wake up regularly like that when he was younger?

T: No, only after a while, maybe since my daughter was born. When he was young, he would stay up late and work if he was in the mood. But as he got older, he mostly worked during the day. Of course, when he had deadlines for movies or television, he worked late at night with his assistants.

O: So, after breakfast, he went into his own room. Did he say something like, "OK, I will go to work" and bring something into his study room?

T: He filled a big teacup—like the ones you get at a sushi restaurant—with green tea and went into his study around nine o'clock. After that he wouldn't come out. I don't know what he was doing inside the room but he did have concentration for his work.

O: So, he didn't come out until he became hungry at lunch time?

T: But he didn't say, "I'm hungry," so around twelve thirty or one o'clock, I called out, "Lunch is ready!" Then he would come out.

O: What did you fix for lunch?

T: For lunch, he liked noodles. He liked *Nagasaki sara-udon*, which is a deep-fried noodle with meat, Chinese cabbage, and fish cake covered with a thick sauce. Other than that, he liked fried noodles, regular udon, and occasionally spaghetti. But he liked Japanese food more than Western food.

O: So he had lunch about twelve thirty or one o'clock, and then went into his room again?

T: Yes, he confined himself in his room. Sometimes he came out to have a tea. But most of the time, he didn't come out until six or seven o'clock. But after he finished dinner, he didn't work anymore. During summer, it was time to watch the baseball games at night.

O: Ah, yes. He was a big fan of the Hanshin Tigers.

Bach Chorale

O: On Takemitsu's working desk, the pencils were all sharpened and lined up from the shortest to the longest. Each eraser had its own place too. Was it like that for a long time?

T: Yes it was.

O: Did he sharpen the pencils and line them up again before he finished the day?

T: That's why they were in order. He could have used another sharpened one after he finished with the first, but instead he sharpened the same one and used it again. [*laughs*]

O: Was it always organized that neatly?

T: He lined up pencils and erasers ever since we lived in Kamakura, about forty years ago. I wonder if that was a habit or his personality. [*laughs*] Mr. Tanikawa wrote a program note for the Tōkyō Symphony Orchestra about this, and there are some photos of it too.

O: I heard that Takemitsu always played a section of Bach's *St. Matthew Passion* on the piano before he started composing. Is that true?

T: Here—I can show you the music score. I brought it with me when I got married. I signed *Asaka Wakayama* over here in the score. Yes, for a certain period, he always played the piece before he started composing.

O: Do you remember when?

T: When we came to Miyota, he always played it. He always brought this score with him.

O: Is that the reason he brought it here?

T: Yes, he didn't play it that much when he was in Tōkyō, but he played it when he was here every time before he began to write a new piece. When he didn't have much time and a deadline was coming up, other people wondered why he didn't start composing right away, but he didn't want to start off too soon. After he decided on the title and opening, he made progress rather quickly; but I think it is difficult for anybody to create something new.

O: Maybe it was necessary to prepare his mind and raise his awareness.

T: I think so. He didn't listen to other music when he was composing. He just played a piece by composers he liked, such as Bach or Debussy,[4] on the piano.

O: Maybe it calmed him down.

T: Yes, and eventually it became like a ceremony. So the purpose of playing Bach's chorale wasn't for any specific musical inspiration, but to settle his mind and appreciate that he can make music. This is my speculation though.

O: Which part of *St. Matthew Passion*? Was it the same section all the time?

---

4 *And then I knew 'twas Wind* (1992) has the same instrumentation as Debussy's *Sonata for flute, viola and harp* (1915).

T: It was the short chorale near the end of the last movement. He liked the last alto aria, where Pedro declaims 'he doesn't know Jesus' three times before the rooster crows.[5]

O: Is there any recorded tape of Takemitsu playing the piano of that part?

T: Of course not! He used to sing a little when he played on the piano.

O: Was he good?

T: No, he wasn't. [*laughs*]

O: But he was playing from his heart?

T: I don't know anything professionally. He wasn't that good and couldn't play smoothly at all, but he had his own particular soft and tender touch. He wouldn't make big, harsh sounds, but I think his tone was clean and beautiful.

O: Besides being an actress, I heard that you were in a choir when you were a student.

T: I actually sang in the KAY choir. It was a joint group from Keisen Girls School, Aoyama Gakuin School, and the YMCA. The YMCA provided the men's voices. Organist, Kōten Okuda[6] was the music teacher of both Keisen and Aoyama School and he formed the choir. The war ended in 1945, and a few years later we sang Handel's *Messiah* at Hibiya Kōkaidō Hall. It was accompanied by the NHK Symphony Orchestra, and conducted by Mr. Kazuo Yamada.

O: Wow, amazing.

---

5 Aria No. 39: "Have mercy Lord, My God, because of this my weeping! Look thou here, Heart and eyes now weep for thee Bitterly." (Trans. by Z. Philip Ambrose)
6 Kōten Okuda (1908-2001): he founded KAY choir in 1947. Their first concert in December 1948 was broadcast through the Far East Network in the U.S.

T: The soloists were Teiichi Nakayama, Mutsumu Shibata, Harue Miyake, and Mr. Shibata's wife, Kiyoko Kubota, was the soprano. We did several choral works together with these soloists. I think we were the first ones to perform *Messiah* after the war. We practiced every week for one year and did *Messiah*; we also did Haydn's *The Creation* with the NHK Symphony, and then the *St. Matthew Passion*.

O: So it was a very high level choir.

T: I think so.

O: Were you a mezzo-soprano?

T: I was a soprano, although now, I don't have a good voice. When we stayed in Toronto, Tōru and I went to hear *Messiah* since it was around the Christmas season. We were talking how bad the chorus was. Even the amateur choirs are pretty good in Japan and we were saying to each other, "Our chorus group sang much better, and NHK Symphony was better, wasn't it?" And then the lady who was sitting next to us started to talk to us in fluent Japanese during the intermission. She said she was a nun who lived in Japan for a while. Probably she couldn't stand the fact that we were bad-mouthing in Japanese and thinking that nobody could understand us. So Tōru and I were so ashamed… Anyway, I don't think Tōru knew much about *St. Matthew Passion*. Since I had the music, he started to play it on the piano.

O: I didn't know that you sang *Messiah*.

T: My parents were both Christian, and ever since I was little, I used to go to Sunday school. I attended Catholic schools such as Rikkyō Girls School ('St. Margaret's School') and Keisen Girls School, so it was natural for me to sing hymns and listen to Western music. Tōru didn't have much contact with those kinds of music. But I heard that he was in a chorus too.[7] He said he sang in Beethoven's Ninth Symphony.

O: I heard that in the Keika Junior High School chorus club, Takemitsu was the leader when the teacher was not around.

---

[7] Takemitsu joined the choir at Keika Junior High School.

T: I see, so he liked music from an early age.

O: I guess so.

T: He was not in an environment that was inclined to music, so I wonder when he started to get involved with music. Not knowing how to begin, he and his friend Hiroyoshi Suzuki[8] went to visit Mr. Kishio Hirai.[9] They wore shabby clothes and *geta*, so they were turned away at the entrance door. [*laughs*]

How did he compose?

O: I heard from Tanikawa that Takemitsu used to say, "I need to be happy in order to compose."

T: Yes, I talked to Mr. Tanikawa about it. When he had any worries or was in an unstable state of mind, he could not compose. So when there was a small quarrel between us, he would say "sorry" to me even though he didn't mean it. He used to say he has to be happy to compose.

O: Is that so.

T: Mr. Tanikawa said that that might be the difference between words and music. Essentially, music is not born from a gloomy feeling, but rather a prayer-like feeling, if not a happy feeling. It is not born from something missing within you, but rather it is born when you are filled with an abundance that is pouring out. In terms of literature, some writers have to suffer tremendously to create their work.

---

[8] Hiroyoshi Suzuki (1931-2006): composer and one of Takemitsu's oldest friends. Takemitsu and Suzuki met in a choir in 1946; Suzuki joined *Jikken Kōbō* in 1951.
[9] Kishio Hirai (1907-53): composer. Takemitsu liked Hirai's *Flute Sonatine* (1941) and decided to visit him in 1947.

O: That's right; it is that way in literature. Sometimes a masterwork is born when the writer is in the depths of agony.

T: Sōseki Natsume's wife was negatively perceived as being a bad wife in the public eye, but personally I don't think she was.[10] I think the writer's wife had a very difficult time. Good literature was often born that way, but music is different. Tōru often said that even Beethoven, who was deaf and was in deep despair, must not have suffered when he was composing. Tōru thought music in general was born from something that moves your heart, such as love, a faint light of hope, even if it was composed in the middle of extreme hardship. It's possible that one can be released from agony by writing, but Tōru said he wasn't that kind of 'artist type.'

O: When Takemitsu started a new piece, did he finish that piece before starting the next one? Or did he compose different works simultaneously?

T: No, he couldn't work on different pieces at the same time. He could write an article on the side, but when it came to composing, the two works interfered with one another, and he could not hear the sound that was coming into his mind. So he was clumsy in that way. There are other composers who can compose two works simultaneously. I have a feeling that it might be related to having a formal music education from early on in life.

O: There are writers who write five different weekly publications and even write a novel on the side. Takemitsu was not like that.

T: Well, if you think of it in a good way, he had the ability to concentrate well. He was searching and searching for his own sound and, I say it again, he didn't have a formal music education! [*laughs*]

---

[10] Sōseki Natsume (1867-1916): the foremost novelist of Japan's Meiji era (1868-1912). His most well known novels include *Kokoro*, *Botchan*, and *I Am a Cat*. Sōseki's son said, "Most of the people who said my mother was a bad wife are not close to my mother."

O: You just said, "the sound coming to his mind." This is my guess but when a composer studies music formally, they don't write what they hear, but write based on the knowledge or what they learned before. In Takemitsu's case, was it like converting an image or concept into sounds and then dictating what he heard in his mind? Do you know how it was like?

T: I don't exactly know how it was. Composing is intellectual work and you need some knowledge, but for him, it seems that the music was coming through his body and his sensitivity…So when he started one work, he would devote himself entirely to it. That type of concentration was amazing, but he couldn't work on two pieces simultaneously. Many people say that Tōru wrote a lot of music and believe that he must have been very busy and stressed, but actually he wasn't that busy. Many people thought so, but actually he wasn't terribly busy and stressed with a lot of work.

O: Did you notice anything about how he composed?

T: Even if I was at his side, I couldn't understand the process of composing. After he was gone, I felt a sense of admiration even more that he could compose a big piece for an orchestra without having formal training. I should've praised him when he was alive. [*laughs*]

O: The titles of his pieces are very unique. I heard that his English titles sometimes came first, but do you know how his titles came about? Do you know how he initially conceived of a piece?

T: When the title was determined, he already decided the overall idea including the instrumentation, what kind of timbre, sometimes even the performers. He drew an illustration or fragments of words in his sketchbook. He was inspired from words and pictures by reading books, and seeing paintings.

O: From other forms of art[11]…

---

[11] Takemitsu's works related to art and literature include *Distance de Fée* (1951) after Shūzo Takiguchi's poem and art book; *Vers, l'arc-en-ciel, Palma* (1984) inspired by

T: Yes, he was influenced by other arts like paintings and literature. He was also moved by the layout and setting of the Japanese garden.[12]

O: I often think that Takemitsu is an 'eye person.' He is very picturesque, and visual.

T: I think so too.

O: I feel that Takemitsu's world is very unique. What I mean by picturesque and visual concerns not only what you can see but also include abstract things and things you cannot see. Sometimes they are whales, water, sea, dream, or fictional things.

T: That's right. I think that's why he liked movies.

O: Tanikawa said that he liked abstract paintings more than concrete paintings, such as those by Renoir or Cézanne.

T: That's right.

O: Was his taste the same in literature?

T: Yes, literature was the same way. He didn't read much of the so-called famous literature, such as Sōseki Natsume. He liked the unusual in novels. He liked Kaizan Nakasato, Jūran Hisao, Kyūsaku Yumeno, Hideo Nakai, and Kyōka Izumi. He read essays, poems, and philosophy more than novels. Among foreign books, he liked surrealistic novels, sci-fi, and detective fiction. I personally like the real detective novels by John Dickson Carr, Agatha Christie, or Freeman Wills Crofts, but Tōru liked fantasy and science fiction. So I guess you can say that his taste is pretty consistent throughout the different art forms.

Miró's paintings; and *Rain Tree* (1981) inspired by Kenzaburō Ōe's short novel "Clever Rain Tree."

[12] Takemitsu's works influenced by gardens include *Arc for strings* (1963), *Dream/Window* (1985), and *Spirit Garden* (1994).

When he is not composing...

O: Did he drink any alcohol at dinner?

T: Everyone thinks he really liked alcohol, but when he was working, he didn't drink at all. Maybe one small can of beer during a hot summer day. He hardly drank alcohol at home.

O: What did he do after dinner?

T: What he was really into were following baseball games on TV or on the radio, reading books, and seeing movies when he had time. But I think he really liked composing the most. I don't have much impression about what he was doing besides that. He liked to get together with his friends and go out with them, but they were considerate and didn't visit us here often when he was working. After he passed away, many friends visited here and stayed overnight, so I think he is envious of us now in heaven.

O: His friends thought they shouldn't interrupt him when he was composing.

T: During the summer, Mr. Tanikawa came here. Sometimes Tōru went for a walk in the evening and had a chat with our neighbors, Hiroshi Mizuo[13] and Kiyoji Ōtsuji,[14] but that was about it. TV arrived here only recently.

O: So, then when he talked about baseball games, was he listening to live coverage on the radio?

T: Yes, yes. Sometimes we could hear Korean radio stations, so when we were listening to the baseball program, the radio would switch from the announcer shouting, "There goes the homerun!" and to something in Korean. [*laughs*] Anyway, we listened to the radio very often,

---

13 Hiroshi Mizuo (1930-): art historian, critic.
14 Kiyoji Ōtsuji (1923-2001): photographer. He participated in *Jikken Kōbō*.

especially morning FM classical music. Since we didn't have TV, we had more time to read books or do something else. When you watch TV, time goes by so quickly. Sometimes we didn't do anything and relaxed, or sometimes we played cards together as a family.

O: Three of you?

T: I found one notebook the other day. The three of us kept a record of playing different games of *hanafuda*[15] and other card games—Old Maid, Seven Bridge, Two Ten Jack. We made a list and kept the score for each of us.

O: Who was good at it?

T: For *hanafuda*, Tōru was the best.

O: Tanikawa and Shūsaku Kawake[16] talked about *mahjong*.

T: Didn't he say that Tōru was a bad player?

O: I heard that Takemitsu was bad at it because he tried to win with special moves and combinations whereas you played to win big.

T: He was not competitive, and he wanted to win with finesses—so in the end he could not win. He really didn't have the desire to compete with anybody. I wanted to win the game, and I liked the kinds of games where one wins or loses.

O: Isn't that part of one's inherent personality? [*laughs*]

T: Maybe so. He didn't fight with many people in his life. [*laughs*] Tōru also liked playing games, but he didn't feel bitter about losing.

---

15 *Hanafuda*: a traditional Japanese card game.
16 Shūsaku Kawake (1952-): TV producer. His mother and Asaka were best friends from since their school days. Takemitsu's family and Kawake's family were long time friends.

O: I heard that you played all night long. Would Takemitsu join you playing overnight?

T: No, he didn't play that long.

O: Because composing was his first thing.

T: I think so. Many people think that being a wife of an artist must be tough or that Tōru must have been in a bad temper at home, but all I needed to do was to prepare meals for him. He was in a good mood when he was composing. It wasn't tough at all.

O: Didn't he get into a bad mood when he was composing?

T: No, not at all. He didn't get into a bad mood or anything.

O: Not even a grimace on his face?

T: He wasn't the type to get anxious or become distressed, even when his compositions were not going so smoothly. Even when a film music deadline was coming up, he actually enjoyed being pressed for time. For film music, he had assistants who stayed over and helped him, and he couldn't be in a bad mood in front of the guests. But even when he was composing alone, he was in a good mood in any type of work. He really loved doing it. He really did.

Loves Pop Music

O: Did Takemitsu hum any particular tunes at home? Was it jazz, popular song, or pop music?

T: Overall it was pop music such as Gilbert O'Sullivan's *Alone Again*, or *Bye Bye Blackbird*, or songs by Crosby, Stills and Nash. He liked old American pop songs. He also liked Japanese popular songs, but he didn't like *enka*.[17]

---

[17] *Enka*: a genre of sentimental ballad music that arose early in the 20th-century.

O: How about jazz?

T: When he was drunk, he used to play jazz on the piano rather than sing.

O: Takemitsu did several sessions with Takeshi Inomata[18] at Sōgetsu Hall in the sixties. Did you go to see these?

T: I sometimes went there. It is a little different trend but Tōru became friends with jazz musicians such as Shōji Suzuki and Rhythm Ace, Sadao Watanabe,[19] Kazumi Watanabe.[20]

O: And pianist Masao Yagi.[21]

T: Yes, yes. Tōru really liked Mr. Yagi, and they worked together on several theater works.

O: The other day, I met Hideto Kanai who is a pioneer Japanese bassist. He told me that Takemitsu wrote him a piece for contrabass and drum.

T: In those days, they were doing a lot of things at Sōgetsu hall.

O: Takemitsu made a pop song CD with Seri Ishikawa.[22]

T: He used to say, "Young people nowadays are singing songs with no melody and no musical soul. They only have rhythm. I want to write a tuneful song." And so he made that CD. The younger people might

---

[18] Takeshi Inomata (1936-): jazz drummer. He premiered Takemitsu's *Three plus Three is Three minus Three* (1961).

[19] Sadao Watanabe (1933-): Japan's leading jazz musician and saxophonist. He premiered Takemitsu's *Good Night* (1960).

[20] Kazumi Watanabe (1953-): jazz guitarist, composer. He joined the world tour of Yellow Magic Orchestra.

[21] Masao Yagi (1932-91): jazz pianist. He premiered several jazz pieces that Takemitsu composed in 1960, and also played for the soundtrack to *White and Black* (1963).

[22] Seri Ishikawa: pop singer, and Yōsui Inoue's wife. She released Takemitsu's pop song album *Tsubasa* (Wings) in 1995, and *MI.YO.TA* in 1997.

think it's too old fashioned, though. In the pop music scene, he liked Keisuke Kuwata.[23]

O: From *Southern All Stars*?

T: Tōru used to say, "Kuwata is amazing, he has great talent." He really respected Paul McCartney and Keisuke Kuwata as great tunesmiths. Tōru was introduced to Yōsui Inoue[24] by Hitoshi Komuro.[25] Yōsui is a unique person, and Tōru liked him a lot. Once they went out to drink and sang Karaoke with him in Shinjuku. He sang the Beatles tunes in front of Yōsui and even tried to sing together and harmonize with him, so I told him to stop! [*laughs*]

O: That must have been a fun way to take his mind off things.

T: He liked people who thought of him as a companion.

O: How did he get in touch with rock musicians? Was it from Maki's CD collections?

T: Foreign musicians like Grateful Dead and David Sylvian were fans of Tōru and came to visit him. Tōru was very happy that they came from foreign countries all over to see him. [*laughs*] Among jazz musicians, there were Keith Jarrett and Chick Corea.

O: Were those musicians fans of Takemitsu, or was Takemitsu a fan of them? Or was it mutual?

T: They heard Tōru's music somewhere and became interested in him, and then they came to see him or wrote letters to him. But sometimes he didn't know the musicians, so Tōru asked Maki who they were. [*laughs*] Some people saw his movie and came into contact with him.

---

[23] Keisuke Kuwata (1956-): a leading Japanese pop singer, and leader of the band *Southern All Stars*.

[24] Yōsui Inoue (1948-): singer songwriter and an important figure in the Japanese music scene.

[25] Hitoshi Komuro (1943-): Japanese folk singer. Takemitsu's song *All Alone* ('*Potsunen*' 1995) was dedicated to Komuro.

O: Was Takemitsu ever influenced by the musicians who visited him?

T: I am not sure… But in fact, he had admiration for those musicians. He said performers are better than composers. And among the performers particularly, he wanted to be like the jazz players. But when it came to writing his own compositions, it is far from that style. [*laughs*] He doesn't have that kind of talent. [*laughs*] Those musicians have good ear, and I think it gave him confidence and fulfillment that those musicians—who had good ears and good rhythm and who lived in present day society—said that his music was "good."

Elementary school days

O: The other day, a friend who was in the same class as Takemitsu from all through their elementary school years came to visit our office, and he told us many things about Takemitsu's childhood. This is the photo from Fujimae Elementary School.

T: Elementary school? I haven't seen this photo before.

O: Takemitsu's nickname was 'forehead' because his forehead was big. He sang really well and took the initiative to sing in the school performances. Takemitsu was the class president, and his friend was the vice president.

T: But I wonder if he had good grades.

O: If he didn't, I don't think he would be elected as a class president. In that elementary school, they chose the president by election.

T: Hmm, I guess he wasn't disliked by others. [*laughs*]

O: In the old days, only students who were both popular and hard working could be the president. His friend, who was vice president, became a Professor of Anatomy at Tōkyō University, so I mentioned that the president and the must be extremely intelligent. He laughed at my comment and said, "Takemitsu was amazing."

T: Oh really. I wish I could chat with him sometime.

O: You always said that Takemitsu never received a proper education, but I imagine that he studied hard and excelled in his youth. Have you heard that kind of a story about him?

T: No, I haven't heard that at all. My mother-in-law didn't talk about that and my sister-in-law always said, "My brother is always in trouble, always in trouble." [*laughs*]

O: His elementary school music teacher took good care of him, and taught him how to play the piano after school. At school, they had a grand piano which was very rare at that time. We found out that the teacher's name is Kyōko Yamamoto.

T: Is that so? I never heard about it.

O: So, it appears that Takemitsu studied music at Keika Junior High School,[26] but maybe his elementary music teacher discovered his talent, and taught him piano and played different kinds of music that could not be taught in the regular music class. As a boy, Takemitsu was able to play at the grand piano when he was in sixth grade.

T: I didn't know about that at all. I heard from him that he liked to sing and he was good at singing. Now I know that he started playing the piano when he was in elementary school. If he didn't know how to play the piano, it would be hard to imagine the sound of the 'paper piano' that he used to carry with him later on. It all makes sense now.

O: I read in an old article that he memorized any piece of music that he only heard once. Did you notice anything about that?

T: Yes, he remembered songs rather quickly. Many musicians are surprisingly tone-deaf, but Tōru might have been a good singer. [*laughs*]

---

26 Keika Junior High School: a private school in Bunkyō ward, Tōkyō. Movie director Akira Kurosawa and conductor Hiyoyuki Iwaki also graduated from this school.

Takemitsu in the center. At a school field trip in 1936.

…Cooking

O: Takemitsu wrote a recipe book when he was in the hospital. Did he cook often?

T: He didn't enjoy cooking that much, but he came here to Miyota alone much of the time, so he had to cook. He would find an article on cooking in a newspaper, or watch a cooking show on TV. When he was in the hospital, he said he couldn't read books and there was nothing good on TV. But he thought that cooking programs were fun to watch. So I think that he was able to take his mind off his illness by writing down recipes on his hospital bed.

O: Cooking is kind of similar to orchestration—gather different materials, combine them, and wonder how it will taste.

T: He said that all the time. Cooking is like orchestration, only using different spices. Many composers like cooking, including Akira Miyoshi[27] and Jōji Yuasa.

O: I wonder if it's similar to writing a score?

T: And he works at home—so cooking can take his mind off from work.

O: What kind of dishes did he make?

T: Nothing extravagant. I only requested things that he could make, so he cooked mostly Japanese style foods, like dried daikon, mushroom soup, and *nattō* (fermented soybeans) soup. His favorite was roasted tofu. When he was in Miyota, he made *ramen* very often. He used instant noodle, and added his own variation, putting meats and vegetables. He used to say, "My noodles are very delicious," so Maki and I asked him to make one for us one time. But he could only cook

---

[27] Akira Miyoshi (1933-): leading Japanese composer. He also wrote recipe books.

for one person at a time, so he had to cook three times. [*laughs*] By the third time, he got bored and wanted to quit. [*laughs*]

O: I would like to try Takemitsu's recipe. I wonder what it will taste like?

T: It's actually pretty good. [*laughs*]

My Room is the Best

O: Takemitsu didn't become a teacher or take any students.

T: If he had become a professor at a college, he would have had a steady, though limited, income, and public schools give pension benefits. When we lived in Shibuya, he was offered a position at a college which had a base salary. It would have been helpful if he had had a steady income, that's for sure. But he said, "I need to travel when I have commissions from abroad, and I want to stay in Miyota when I compose. If I have to go to school several times a week, my composing will be interrupted. And, I like spending time with young people, so if I become a teacher, I will be totally absorbed in it." [*laughs*] So he turned down the offer saying, "I can't do it. First and foremost, I don't have proper education, so I cannot teach other people." And then they said, "When you go abroad, you can cancel the class, so you can come and teach when you can." After hearing that, Tōru got mad: "What do you mean? That is totally irresponsible. What are the students going to do if the teacher is not there often?!" He started to get really angry. [*laughs*] He was not going to accept it anyway, so he didn't have to say it like that. [*laughs*]

O: Takemitsu has been a visiting professor in U.S.

T: Yes, he was invited by Yale University.[28] Even at that time, I wasn't so positive about it because he couldn't work for three months and

---

[28] Takemitsu was invited as a guest lecturer to Yale University in January of 1975 and stayed for three months. He received the prestigious Sanford Award during his

consequently had no income. But he said, "After I arrive there, I will have a salary right away, and then I can send it to you." So I let him have some money and sent him off to the U.S. I waited and waited, but I didn't receive any money from him. I found out later that he received lump sum money from the university, but he used it all up and had no money when he came home to Japan! I heard that he was quite popular at Yale. Every Saturday, he would bring his students to New York from New Haven, stay at a hotel, and see a movie and drink. No wonder he was so popular. [*laughs*] Over there, only a couple of students were taking lessons from him, and lessons didn't mean he was teaching. They would just discuss the work that the students brought, and then go to New York on weekends. [*laughs*]

O: Isn't that called 'composer-in-residence'? He was invited several times to participate in events abroad for a certain period of time.

T: Besides Yale University, he received invitations from the University of California to be a composer-in-residence for a long-term visit. He went for many short visits to music festivals as a theme composer. One really long stay was when we went to Toronto after the premiere of *November Steps*. The Rockefeller Foundation was going to support us financially for one year. This time our whole family went together. We were told to be there at least nine months, but Tōru said he couldn't stay that long, and we came back to Japan after seven months. After the concert in New York, we stayed at Mr. Ozawa's house in Canada for about two months, but he said, "I want to go home." He couldn't compose when he was traveling or living in a temporary housing. He had to be home. He was told that he didn't have to compose in New York and all he had to do was go to concerts and meet other composers, but he wasn't interested in those things. He said, "I want to go home soon. Let's go home." So we decided to come home sooner than planned. But that was our first foreign experience, so we planned to travel to Europe before going back. And when we arrived in Paris, he said, "I absolutely want to go home now." At that time, our artist friend Mitsuo Kanō suggested that we travel Italy, Spain or Belgium, but Tōru said, "Definitely not, I want to go home now. I will buy you

---

residency, and was the second Japanese to receive the award. The first was Hideo Saitō, the teacher of Seiji Ozawa at Tōhō School of Music.

nice clothes with the travel money. So let's go home." So he bought me fake Channel suits and we came home to Japan.

O: I wonder if he can't get inspired unless he is in a Japanese cultural climate.

T: No, it's not just the climate. He had to be in his own house and own room. He had a ritual when he used to compose—he pours green tea in his big teacup, brings that into his study, sits in front of his piano, and so forth. It doesn't matter if his family is there or not. When I was in Miyota, we talked too much and played around, so he would say, "Why don't you go back to Tōkyō?" [*laughs*] When he wasn't in the mood, he often went out for a walk. He would stroll around near the house in Miyota and when we were in Lake Tama. I noticed that he smoked when he came back from his walk. He didn't smoke inside the house, but he was smoking outside. I realized that the reason for him taking a walk was to smoke behind my back. [*laughs*]

Cook, the cat. 1973.

Cook, the cat

O: I'm moving on to the next topic: Cats. [*laughs*] I am a cat lover, so I really need to ask you this: [*laughs*] All the Takemitsu family members love cats, is that right? When you were first married, you didn't have cats yet.

T: When we lived in Kamakura, we rented a cottage next to the main house, and the owner had a cat. I really liked the cat, but Tōru didn't care for it that much. When Maki was little, she didn't have siblings, and she started asking about getting a pet. Since we lived in an apartment we could not have dogs, so we decided to get a cat. Our neighbor Heihachirō Mita, who played bassoon in the NHK Symphony, had many cats. He gave us a newborn kitty. We named him 'Cook.'

O: In the first volume of the *Complete Takemitsu Edition*, there is a photo of Takemitsu with a cat, that is Cook, isn't it?

T: Yes it is. At first he said that Cook is not allowed in his room and on the dining table. But he fell in love with Cook right away. When Cook jumped on the chair next to him when we were eating, he picked him up and let him eat in his arm. [*laughs*] When he traveled abroad, he called us right away and asked, "Can you put Cook on the phone? How is he doing?" And I said, "I think he knows that it's you on the phone." Then he said, "Really!" and sounded happy. [*laughs*] At the end, Tōru took care of Cook's breakfast. When the meal was late, Cook would go to Tōru's room or even followed him to the bathroom. He said, "Ah, you were waiting for daddy, huh." He has never called himself "Daddy" or "Papa," not even in front of his own daughter.

O: Did Cook go into Takemitsu's composing room?

T: Sure he did. Tōru left the piano lid open, so sometimes we heard him walking on the piano in the middle of the night. He didn't get mad at Cook. Maki listened to Cook's piano playing, and said, "Well, it is not that different from Daddy's piece." [*laughs*] Tōru talked to Cook saying, "You are the only one who really understands me." When hospitalized, a patient usually brings in photos of their family, right? Tōru didn't bring his family photos, but he brought Cook's photo. Since he was hospitalized for six months, he was worried that Cook might not remember him. After he was discharged and came home, Cook started to ask for food from him, and he said, "Good, you remembered Daddy." [*laughs*] I didn't think he would become so attached to Cook.

Listening to *St. Matthew Passion* before his passing…

O: Did you think that Takemitsu would recover when he was discharged from the hospital the first time?[29]

T: If you ask me that, I am not sure… I had mixed feelings about it. On one hand, I thought he would be alright, but at the same time, I had uneasiness. Tōru didn't say to me that he might not make it. But he confided in Maki, "I wonder if I will really recover…" The doctor was rather optimistic and said he would be all right. When he was discharged, Tōru was wondering if he was cured and said, "I want more time, at least three more years, or five years at most. If I had three years, I can finish the opera." If he had felt even a bit insecure, he would've discussed our future together, but we never talked about it. We tried to believe that he would recover, and didn't touch the subject.

O: I see…

T: After being discharged from the hospital in October of 1995, he recuperated here in Miyota, and was doing well writing guitar and flute pieces. After the New Year, he suddenly came down with a fever on January 15th, and was hospitalized again. We thought that collagen disease developed again. But the doctor told me in his room that the cancer had moved to a part of the liver that could not be operated upon. After I went back to the hospital room, he was contemplative for a while, but he appeared to be calm and kept his presence of mind I

---

[29] Takemitsu was diagnosed with colon cancer and was hospitalized in April 1995. He was discharged in October, and recuperated in Miyota.

was the one who burst out in tears. It was a terrible thing to do. In this kind of situation, the wife has to remain strong and be supportive, but my mind went blank and I lost my composure. Then Tōru sat up in upright position and said, "It is OK. I will try my best. Chemo-therapy worked pretty well the last time." He was the one cheering me up.

O: Since he was unable to undergo surgery, chemotherapy was the only choice of treatment left for him…

T: When he started chemo, his white blood cell count suddenly dropped. Since he was susceptible to getting infected by other diseases, he was transferred to the intensive care unit. He was hospitalized on January 15th, started chemo at the beginning of February, then he quarantined in a bio-clean room for ten days. Prior to that, many people came to visit, but no one came during those ten days. When I went to see him, I had to get sanitized and wear a white gown. The doctor was giving him medication to increase the number of white blood cells, and as long as the count returned to normal, the doctor said he should be alright. Tōru was calm and had good appetite, so I thought the treatment was going well. When I think back now, the situation was quite severe, but I was too optimistic…or rather I wanted to stay hopeful. When I visited him, he usually sat up and started talking immediately, but the day before he passed away, he just lay on the bed and said, "hi…"

O: That was February 19th.

T: Yes. Dinner was delivered to the room and he tried to sit up, but he was surprised that he didn't have the strength to support himself. When I tried to help him, he said, "I don't think you can help me." So he grabbed a hold of the bed frame and the IV bar and got out of bed by himself. He sat on the chair firmly and said, "The rice porridge is well cooked today" and he finished a small bowl of porridge. I said, "See you tomorrow" and left the room. But at five in the morning, I received a call from the hospital saying that his condition had worsened suddenly, so I told Maki to call the hospital and sent her there. It was before the first train started to run, so I was thinking of driving to the hospital, but Maki told me, "Mom, don't drive to the hospital. Please wait for the first train." So I jumped on the first train and went to the hospital. It was the longest forty-minute ride from Higashi-Murayama to Shinjuku. When I arrived at the hospital, Tōru was already unconscious. I heard that when Maki arrived, she called out "Tōru saaan!" and he shed tears, so maybe he understood. He had developed pneumonia but he had the respirator on, and the doctor said things should be OK, if he can overcome this. Maki was thinking of reserving a hotel nearby and we hadn't eaten anything, so we left the room and walked to the elevator. Then the doctor suddenly came running after us and said, "His blood pressure plummeted suddenly, so please come back immediately." When we went back to the room, his blood pressure went down all of a sudden, and then…

His condition didn't look that bad to me until then. On the 17th, two days before he died, the weather forecast said Tōkyō might have an unusual, heavy snow. Tōru was worried that I could not go back to Higashi-Murayama, so he told me not to come the next day. I was tired, so I took a day off which I hadn't done in a long time.

O: That was the 18th, and at the night of the 17th, Tōkyō had an unusual, heavy snow.

T: Yes. On that night, Tōru was able to listen to the entire *St. Matthew Passion* on NHK's FM radio station. It is an interesting thing. If I had been by his bedside, he wouldn't have turned on the radio. It just happened to be the day that I'd decided to take off, and noone came to see him because of the snow. When he turned on the radio, *St. Matthew Passion* was playing. It was snowing all day with so little noise from outside, and he was able to listen to his favorite *St. Matthew Passion* all by himself with a quiet state of mind.

O: It is really rare for FM radio to play *St. Matthew Passion* in its entirety.

T: When I visited him at the hospital on the 19th, he said to me, "I listened to the entire *St. Matthew Passion* on the radio yesterday. Wow, Bach is really great. I am not Christian but it really is something…" He was really calm and peaceful. Probably he knew how serious his illness was at that point. I think that by listening to *St. Matthew Passion*, he was in the state of mind to just let go, and devote his life to something greater. I couldn't help but wonder if that piece showed him the way to a quiet path to his next journey and a grace from God.

At CineMusic Festival in Switzerland. March 1995.

Chapter 6

Music through Friendship

This portion of interview was conducted in May 2010 at the Takemitsu cottage in Miyota. Mitsuko Ono interviewed Asaka-san about Takemitsu's friends, most importantly Simon Rattle and David Raksin, from abroad.

Music through Friendship

Mitsuko Ono: Tōru Takemitsu became good friends with many foreign musicians and artists. Since these interviews are now being published in English, I would like to ask you a bit more about Takemitsu's relationship with his friends.

Asaka Takemitsu: Because I was a wife of a composer, I attended many concerts and festivals with Tōru. I have many good memories with those people we encountered through these occasions.

O: Takemitsu did not cut off and end his relationships with artists whom he met at festivals or performances. He maintained his relationship and friendships for a long time, didn't he?

T: Yes, Tōru had a lasting relationship with friends from many different occasions.

O: And it wasn't limited to musicians.

T: Tōru had many painter and artist friends who were fond of music, such as Jasper Johns and Isamu Noguchi. Jasper was friends with John Cage and they had a good relationship, artistically and personally. So they were doing something similar to what Tōru and other Japanese were doing at *Jikken Kōbō*. They were trying to find out how to create a present culture or a new culture, from just as a musician's point of view…

O: It was their common ideal…

T: Yes, that was their common ideal, so they became really closer. I don't know what they thought about Tōru's music, but they had a special bond between them, and I think Tōru was fortunate to have many opportunities.

O: Takemitsu was able to maintain these relationships because he traveled abroad often. If he were to stay in Japan, he could not meet foreign artists that easily.

T: That's right…

…

O: Takemitsu met Simon Rattle[1]—who now has the title of "Sir"—a long time ago.

---

[1] Simon Rattle (1955-): British conductor. He was the conductor of City of Birmingham Symphony, and is presently the principal conductor at Berlin Philharmonic.

T: Yes, they knew each other since they were young. The first time I met him was when they did *riverrun* (1984) in Los Angeles. After the concert was over, we made plans to meet at the airport and flew to New York together. Simon had on a T-shirt and a pair of jeans, and was carrying a backpack and holding his baby son. He looked just like one of the young people in L.A. Simon wasn't conservative but more easy going.

O: Mr. Rattle also likes movies, I heard.

T: Yes, yes.

O: Even B-rated or C-rated movies.

T: That's right! I guess Tōru and Simon hit off in that respect too.

O: They met when Simon was the principal conductor at the City of Birmingham Orchestra. Did they perform *riverrun* in New York?

T: Yes, they performed *riverrun* and Mahler at Carnegie Hall.

O: Mr. Rattle premiered several works by Takemitsu: *Vers, l'arc-en-ciel, Palma* (1984), *riverrun* (1984), *My Way of Life –In Memory of Michael Vyner* (1990).

T: The poem for *My Way of Life* is written by Ryūichi Tamura[2] and I went to the premiere together with Tōru. That was the time when Tōru's music was getting criticized for being too sweet or for returning to tonality. I was at the rehearsal, and I also thought this piece was rather sweet, and I talked to him. He said, "It's OK to be this way sometimes, but not all the time, I hope. Sometimes we can have something sweet." [*laughs*] Anyway, there are so many other talented composers out there but Simon Rattle and wonderful ensembles like London Sinfonietta chose his music to perform, so Tōru was really lucky.

---

[2] Ryūichi Tamura (1923-98): Japanese poet, essayist, translator of English novels.

...

O: The last foreign country Takemitsu visited was Switzerland, wasn't it?

T: Yes. There was a movie music festival called CineMusic Festival in Gstaad in 1995, and we met...

O: David Raksin?

T: Yes! You know it's funny. He is much older than Tōru, but they got along right away, just like they were old friends. Raksin is a film composer in U.S., and Tōru saw a lot of American films, especially the ones right after the war.

O: It was during his childhood, so I guess it's imprinted on him.

T: Raksin was proud of working with Charles Chaplin, and told Tōru that Charlie used to say this and that. Tōru listened to him with much curiosity. Raksin composed a lot of film music, but became really famous for the music for *Laura* (1944). Tōru of course had heard of him, but that was the first time he met him. But Raksin was so nice to Tōru as if he were his real son. When Maki and I were about to return to Tōkyō, Raksin said, "I will take Tōru to L.A. with me," and so they flew together. Raksin recommended Tōru for the Film Music Society's Career Achievement Award and took him to the award ceremony and other parties with him. Raksin was so good to Tōru.

O: I guess they shared many common interests.

T: Soon after he came back to Japan, Tōru was hospitalized at Toranomon Hospital in Tōkyō. The doctor needed to examine his bladder tissue so he went into the anesthetic room to have a partial anesthesia. At the hospital, background music was playing, and what Tōru heard in the room was the music of *Laura*. Tōru was shocked! He had never heard Raksin's music on any other occasions, and now suddenly he hears Raksin's music right after they had spent time together. He couldn't believe it and said to me later, "Asaka-san,

Asaka-san! The music I heard at the anesthetic room was the theme music of *Laura*!" Isn't it interesting?

O: I don't normally drive my car, but when I turned on the engine today, Takemitsu's music was playing on the radio! [*laughs*]

T: See, it's interesting. There is so much music out there, and suddenly Tōru hears the music by someone that he feels so close to…

…

T: The last time we met Messiaen was at the premiere of *A String Around Autumn* (1989) with Ms. Nobuko Imai as the soloist and Kent Nagano as the conductor. Messiaen came to listen to the performance and praised his orchestration saying, "Others cannot do this kind of orchestration. It was wonderful." Messiaen's compliment gave Tōru more confidence in what he had been doing. Tōru was so happy that a great master said his music was good. He was always bragging about that. [*laughs*]

O: I see. Messiaen first visited Japan in 1962, but do you know when they first met each other?

T: I don't think they met during Messiaen's first visit to Japan.

O: When Takemitsu attended the Cannes Festival for the music of *Kwaidan* (1965), it looks like they met each other in Paris. And for the recording of *November Steps* with the Toronto Symphony in 1967 with RCA, it was coupled with Messiaen's *Turangalïila Symphony*, so they might have met at the recording session.

T: Some time later in 1974 or 75, when Peter Serkin's group Tashi was playing *Quartet for the End of Time* in New York, Tōru had a lesson with Messiaen. When I think back, I wish I had asked him more about how he composed, even though it might have been difficult for him to explain it. And I should've acknowledged his hardwork and paid more compliments like, "That sounds wonderful!" rather than simply saying, "I guess it's good." [*laughs*]

O: Maybe it was better that way, as opposed to always keeping an eye on his back.

T: When Tōru asked, "Can you listen to this for a minute?" Maki and I looked at each other and rolled our eyes. We didn't know what to say, you know? He starts out playing the piano which didn't sound so great and says, "It goes this way, and here comes the flute. Fuuuuu" and he hummed the flute melody by himself. [*laughs*]

Deepening Artistry

O: For instance, in the case of performers Robin Engelman and John Wyre—who became close to Takemitsu—it appears to me that they had a desire to be challenged by Takemitsu's music. Takemitsu's use of percussion in his music is unique, isn't it?

T: Yes, I agree. Tōru didn't use percussion the same way as they would in a traditional orchestra. He often said he had hopes to make the percussion loud and substantial, but he couldn't do it. It wasn't his cup of tea. He said he doesn't have that kind of sound in his own music.

O: I see.

T: Tōru then got to know Japanese percussionists such as Yasunori Yamaguchi and Sumire Yoshihara who created subtle and sensitive sounds, different from those of the foreign percussionists. After that, Engelman met Yamaguchi through Tōru later on. By meeting the performers, Tōru learned many techniques and realized the unlimited possibilities of each instrument. And he was able to deepen his spirituality and artistry through interaction with the performers. Tōru really learned a lot from them.

O: Takemitsu often used English titles alongside Japanese titles when he presented his new works. Of course one big reason is that the commissions were often from abroad. Do you think he put a special importance to his relationships outside Japan? For example, when he started *Music Today* Festival, he didn't just do things with Japanese performers but he brought Peter Serkin and others whom he met abroad, or he created a special music session with Yūji Takahashi and so forth. His creative juices were flowing all over.

T: Well, I don't think he was thinking so much about a mission to connect with foreign artists, it was more like he wasn't so conscious about it. He didn't think he needed to invite musicians from any particular country. If there was a good performer in France, he would go for France, and if one was in the U.S., then he would go for U.S. Maybe it has to do with him not attending a music school, so when he first started out as a composer, he wasn't tied up in a teacher-pupil relationship. When you look at the Japanese music society—I think the same goes with other fields in Japan—there is often a strong teacher-disciple relationship. But Tōru did not belong to any of the academic establishments, so he wasn't influenced by the traditional institutional relationships. He was free to choose what he liked without being bound by the country or by convention.

O: When Takemitsu encountered performers with common sensibilities or common interests, I guess it didn't matter to him whether they were Japanese or British or American.

T: Tōru's friends had interests not only in music but also in other regular things. Tōru met many people with whom he hit it off initially as a person, even before talking about music. Little did he dream that his music would be performed time and again after his death. He had never dreamed of it!

O: [*laughs*]

T: When I think back, I think Tōru was a very lucky person. He had so many good friends, and he was able to compose with joy. When he went to festivals and spoke with the judges and others, he really enjoyed the whole process. He never thought of his job as a loathsome thing.

O: That should be a pleasant experience for people surrounding him. It will extend his circle of good friendship.

155

T: That's right. When I have to talk to foreigners, I feel small, mainly because I do not speak foreign languages. But Tōru had a dignified manner, not arrogant, even when he was standing next to a tall person. He didn't care that he was short, yet he didn't think highly of himself either. He was a strange person in a way. There are so many other things I want to ask him if he were still here with me today. [*laughs*]

Tōru and Asaka Takemitsu Chronology

Tōru Takemitsu's age is given in parentheses.
Entries marked with an * refer specifically to Asaka

1930 (0)   Born October 8th in Hongō, Tōkyō, as the first son of Takeo and Reiko Takemitsu. One month after his birth, Tōru and his mother move to Dalian, China where his father is employed.

1934 (4)   *Asaka (Wakayama) moves to Setagaya-Daita with her family.

1937 (7)   Tōru returns to Japan by plane and resides at his uncle's house in Hongō, Tōkyō. Enters Fujimae Elementary school.

1938 (8)   **March**: Tōru's father dies of tuberculosis in his hometown in Kagoshima.

1941 (11)   **April**: *Asaka enters Rikkyō Girls School.

1943 (13)   **April**: Tōru enters Keika Junior High School.

1944 (14)   Tōru moves to Komagome Tōkyō, and lives with his mother. *Asaka's parents move to a suburb to avoid war damage; she stays with her elder sister and her husband in Setagaya, Tōkyō.

1945 (15)   **March**: Tōru's mother's and uncle's houses are destroyed in the fire-bombing of Tōkyō.
April: Tōru move to Saitama prefecture for army mobilization. Listens to Lucienne Boyer's *Parles-moi d'amour*, which leaves an indelible impression. He resolves to pursue composition after the end of the war.
*Asaka works at the 'school factory' until the end of the war, August 15th.

1946 (16)   Tōru's family moves to Setagaya-Daita. Develops first symptoms of tuberculosis. Sells cigarettes on the black market for the occupation forces. Joins choral group of Noriaki Hamada.
December: Starts working as a band boy in at the US Army camp in Yokohama.
*Asaka enters Keisen Girls School and joins a drama club. She later joins the KAY chorus and sings *Messiah*, *The Creation* and *St. Matthew Passion*.

1947 (17)   After hearing Kishio Hirao's *Flute Sonatine*, Tōru asks to be taken
on as Hirao's pupil, but is rejected. Rents his first piano. Hardly
attends school at this time.

1948 (18)   **June**: Studies informally with Yasuji Kiyose, who introduces him
to Fumio Hayasaka. Tuberculosis grows worse.
*Asaka graduates from Keisen Girls School.

1949 (19)   Tōru graduates from Keika High School.
*Asaka auditions for Haiyūza Actors Studio, and discovers that
she has tuberculosis at the medical examination.

1950 (20)   Tōru encounters Asaka, the elder sister of his friend Shigeto,
who lives near his house.
March: Meets Shōzō Kitadai and Katsuhiro Yamaguchi at the
LP record concert of CIE (Civil Information and Education
Section).
October: Joins *Shin-Sakkyokuha Kyōkai* ('Association of New
School of Composition'), but leaves two years later. Introduced
to poet/art critic Shūzō Takiguchi by Kitadai.
December: Premiere of *Lento in Due Movimenti*. After the concert,
meets Kuniharu Akiyama and Jōji Yuasa backstage. *Lento* is
criticized as "pre-music" by music critic Ginji Yamane.

1951 (21)   **May**: Premiere of *Distance de Fée*, inspired by a Shūzō Takiguchi's
poem.
September: Joins *Jikken Kōbō* ('Experimental Workshop'), an
interdisciplinary artistic group founded by Takiguchi.
November: First concert of *Jikken Kōbō*. Premiere of Ballet, *Joy
of Life* ('Ikiru Yorokobi').

1952 (22)   **August**: Premiere of *Uninterrupted Rest*.

1953 (23)   ***April**: Asaka takes role of narrator in Takemitsu's ballet *A Trip
on the Galactic Railway* ('Gingatetsudō no Tabi'). Helps copy
scores for Tōru.
June: Diagnosed with tuberculosis, Tōru enters Keiō Hospital,
and returns his rented piano. Becomes acquainted with Shuntarō
Tanikawa, who visits him at the hospital.

1954 (24)   **March**: Leaves the hospital before recovering fully, and begins
living with Asaka in Senzoku-Ike, Ōta ward, Tōkyō. Becomes

friends with his next door neighbor, Heihachirō Mita, a
bassoonist in the NHK Symphony Orchestra.
June 15th: Marries Asaka. Friends gather to celebrate.
Upright piano delivered unexpectedly by Toshirō Mayuzumi.

1955 (25)   **March**: Composes music for the radio program *Four Seasons of
Sound* ('Oto no Shiki') directed by Naoya Yoshida, and continues
collaborating with him.
October: Moves to Sasuke, Kamakura to recuperate. Members
of *Jikken Kōbō* and other friends visit his house often. Despite
tubercolosis, composes music for the radio drama *Flame* ('Honō').
Fumio Hayasaka dies from tuberculosis.
Tōru and Asaka encounter Yūji Takahashi in a train on the
Yokosuka Line.

1956 (26)   **February**: Premiere broadcast of tape-music pieces *Vocalism A·I,
Clap Vocalism, Tree-Sky-Bird* ('Ki-Sora-Tori').
July: Composes first film score (in collaboration with Masaru
Satō) for *Crazed Fruit* ('Kurutta Kajitsu'). directed by Kō
Nakahira.
August: First film score with Shōchiku Films for *Red and Green*
('Shu to Midori') directed by Noboru Nakamura. (Recommended
for the job by Toshirō Mayuzumi). Subsequently scores many
films for Shōchiku.

1957 (27)   Battles tuberculosis; often seriously ill.
June: Premiere of *Requiem for Strings* (Masashi Ueda conducting
the Tōkyō Symphony Orchestra.)

1958 (28)   Illness gradually improves.
August: Awarded first prize at the *2nd Festival of Contemporary
Music* in Karuizawa for *Le Son Calligraphié 1*.

1959 (29)   **January**: Becomes a member of *20 Seiki Ongaku Kenkyūjo* ('20th
Century Music Research Institute').
April: Igor Stravinsky visits Japan and praises Takemitsu's
Requiem for Strings. Tōru and Asaka invited to lunch with
Stravinsky.

1960 (30)   **January**: Composes *Quiet Design* (for tape) in collaboration with
Asaka.
April: Premiere of *Water Music* (for tape) and *Landscape* for string
quartet at *The Tōru Takemitsu Exhibition* as part of the second

regular meeting of *Sakkyokuka Shūdan* ('Group of Composers') at
Sōgetsu Art Center Art Center.
July: Hospitalized for fatigue at the Shōnan Sanatorium in
Kotsubo, Zushi city.
December: Moves to Fujimichō, Chiyoda-ward, Tōkyō.

1961 (31)   **March**: Argues with director Susumu Hani during the making of
Bad Boys ('Furyō Shōnen'), but continues his fascination with film
music.
April: Premiere of *Piano Distance* (piano: Yūji Takahashi).
August: Premiere of *RING*, conducted by Seiji Ozawa; becomes
acquainted with Ozawa. *RING* receives the German
Ambassador's Prize.
September: Moves to Omotemachi Akasaka, Minato-ward,
Tōkyō, located conveniently near Sōgetsu Art Center.
December: Birth of daughter Maki ('real tree'), named after
Takemitsu's composition *Music of Trees* ('Ki no Kyoku').

1962 (32)   **October**: Participates in *Sapporo Contemporary Music Festival* with
John Cage, who is visiting Japan.
Composes film scores for *The Inheritance* and *Harakiri* (both
directed by Masaki Kobayashi), and *The Pitfall* (directed by
Hiroshi Teshigahara).

1963 (33)   **January**: Moves to Seijō, Setagaya-ward, Tōkyō owing
construction noise from the Tōkyō Olympics. Becomes friends
with Yasushi Akutagawa and Kenzaburō Ōe who live near his
house.

1964 (34)   **March**: Invited to the *Festival of Arts in this Century*, organized by
the East-West Center of Hawaii. The Takemitsu family travels
abroad for the first time. Tōru continues on to San Francisco
alone, and meets Sam Francis and Jasper Johns at a David Tudor
concert.
Asks Katsuya Yokoyama to play shakuhachi for the score to *The
Assassin*, directed by Masahiro Shinoda, and Kinshi Tsuruta to
play biwa for *Kwaidan*, directed by Masaki Kobayashi.
Composes music for twelve movies, including *Woman in the
Dunes*, directed by Hiroshi Teshigahara.

1965 (35)   ***May**: Asaka hospitalized in Toranomon Hospital in Tōkyō.
June: Receives UNESCO International Music Council's Best
Composition Award for *Textures*, leading to global recognition.

Tōru and Asaka purchase a cottage in Miyota, a mountain villa in Kitasaku District, Nagano Prefecture.

1966 (36) **May**: Plans and organizes the contemporary music festival *Orchestral Space* with Toshi Ichiyanagi. Premiere of *Arc* (piano: Yūji Takahashi, with the Yomiuri Nippon Symphony Orchestra, Seiji Ozawa conducting) and *Eclipse* (biwa: Kinshi Tsuruta, shakuhachi: Katsuya Yokoyama).
June: Film score for *The Kii River* ('Ki no Kawa'), directed by Noboru Nakamura. Last score for Shōchiku studios, owing to argument about music in the wedding scene; yet wins 16th Mainichi Film Award for his music to this film.
August: RCA Victor releases four LP box sets, "The Music of Tōru Takemitsu."

1967 (37) **February**: Premiere of *Dorian Horizon* commissioned by the Serge Koussevitzky Foundation (Aaron Copland conducting the San Francisco Symphony Orchestra); awarded Music Critics prize for this work.
October: Takemitsu family travels to Toronto and New York for six months on a Rockefeller Foundation grant. While in Toronto, resides at Seiji Ozawa's home.
November: Premiere of *November Steps* for biwa, shakuhachi and orchestra (biwa: Kinshi Tsuruta, shakuhachi: Katsuya Yokoyama, Seiji Ozawa conducting the New York Philharmonic), commissioned by the New York Philharmonic for its 125th anniversary.
December: Performance and recording of *November Steps* in Toronto, (Seiji Ozawa conducting the Toronto Symphony Orchestra).

1968 (38) **March**: Moves to Higashiyama, Meguro-ward, Tōkyō.

1969 (39) **January**: Premiere of *Asterism* (piano: Yūji Takahashi, Seiji Ozawa conducting the Toronto Symphony Orchestra). Toronto Symphony performs Takemitsu's works during two-week celebration. Takemitsu family stays in Toronto.
October: Composer-in-Residence at *Canberra Spring Festival* of Musica Viva, Australia.

1970 (40) **August**: Organizes contemporary music festival *Konnichi no Ongaku* ('Music Today') at the Space Theater of Expo '70 in Osaka.

Moves to Udagawachō, Shibuya-ward, Tōkyō. The families of
Jōji Yuasa and Toshi Ichiyanagi move into the same
condominium.

1971 (41) **June**: Film score for *The Ceremony* ('Gishiki'), directed by Nagisa
Ōshima.
August: Travels with his family to the *Marlboro Music Festival*;
meets Peter Serkin and they become good friends.
October: Thirty-seven of Takemitsu's works are introduced at
the *Contemporary Music Days Festival* of the *International Music Week
in Paris (SMIP)*, the first French festival to feature Takemitsu's
music.
Publishes essay collection *Sound: Confronting the Silence* ('Oto,
Chinmoku to Hakariaeru Hodoni') .

1972 (42) **December**: Visits Bali with Xenakis, Betsy Jolas, Maurice
Fleuret and other French musicians. Asaka and Maki come along.
Takemitsu is impressed with traditional Balanese music.

1973 (43) **May**: Composer-in-Residence at London Music Digest; eleven
works performed. Plans and organizes the annual contemporary
music festival *Music Today* in commemoration of the opening of
Seibu Theater in Shibuya. (Continues organizing this yearly
festival until 1992.)
August: Privately publishes an autobiographical novel *Bone Moon,
or a 'Honeymoon'* ('Kotsugetsu—aruiwa 'honey moon''), and
dedicates this to Asaka.
Bassoonist Heihachirō Mita gives a cat to the Takemitsu family.
The cat is named 'Cook' after *Captain Cook*.

1974 (44) **July**: Premiere of *Folios* commissioned by Kiyoshi Shōmura.

1975 (45) **January**: Visiting professor at Yale University in U.S. Receives
Sanford Medal.
September: Premiere of *Quatrain* (Tashi, with Seiji Ozawa
conducting the New Japan Philharmonic Orchestra).
December: Moves to Tamakochō, Higashimurayama city,
Tōkyō along with Yuasa family.

1976 (46) **February**: Receives Otaka Prize, for the orchestral work
Quatrain.

1977 (47)   **June**: Release of LP "Twelve Songs: The Earth is Smiling" (guitar: Kiyoshi Shōmura). *Asaka helps with the selection of songs.
November: Premiere of *A Flock Descends into the Pentagonal Garden* (Edo de Waart conducting the San Francisco Symphony)

1978 (48)   **October**: Travels to Paris as an artistic advisor for *Festival d'Automne à Paris* (Paris Autumn Festival), and organizes eighteen concerts of "Traditional and modern music of Japan" as part of the exhibition *MA-Espace-temps au Japon*, (Ma, Space-Time of Japan) directed by the architect Arata Isozaki.
December: Film score for *Glowing Autumn* ('Moeru Aki') directed by Masaki Kobayashi.

1979 (49)   **April**: Family sends letter of protest to president of the Hanshin Tigers regarding the release of Kōichi Tabuchi, a famous pitcher for the team.
July: Shūzō Takiguchi passes away; composes *Les yeux clos* in memory.

1980 (50)   **March**: Composer-in Residence at the *Vancouver Festival of Contemporary Music*.
May: Premiere of *Far calls. Coming, far!* (Violin: Ida Kavafian, Tadaaki Otaka conducting the Tōkyō Metropolitan Symphony Orchestra). Dedicates this work to his daughter Maki.
August: Visits Groute Eylandt, Australia for a Eurovision project with Jiri Kylian. Takemitsu is impressed by the culture and myths of the Australian aborigines.

1981 (51)   **March**: Regent's Lecturer at the University of California at San Diego.
September: Guest Composer at Berliner Festwochen "Japan in Berlin."
Receives many invitations from foreign universities and music festivals from this point on.

1983 (53)   **April** to **June**: Lectures at Harvard and Yale Universities, and University of Colorado.
June: Mother dies at the age of 78.

1984 (54)   **March**: Dedicates collection of movie essays, *Quotation of Dream* ('Yume no Inyō'), to Asaka.

June: Composer-in-Residence at the *Aldeburgh Festival* of Music and the Arts.

1985 (55)   **January**: Premiere of *riverrun* (piano: Peter Serkin, Simon Rattle conducting the Los Angeles Philharmonic).
May: Receives *Ordre des Arts et des Lettres* (Order of Arts and Letters) from the French Government.
June: Composes film score for *Ran* directed by Akira Kurosawa; but they have major conflicts over the score.

1986 (56)   **October**: Appointed as a supervisor of the Suntory Hall *International Program for Music Composition* (Continues involvement in subsequent years). BBC airs the documentary, "Thirteen Steps around Tōru Takemitsu."

1987 (57)   **February**: Wins Los Angeles Film Critics Award for the score to *Ran*.
Commissioned by the Opéra National de Lyon.

1988 (58)   **May**: Premiere of *Tree Line* (Oliver Knussen conducting the London Sinfonietta).
July: Serves on adviser committee to the 1st *New York International Festival of the Arts*; organizes four concerts at the Japan Society, New York.

1989 (59)   **November**: Premiere of *A String Around Autumn*, commissioned by the *Festival d'Automne à Paris* as part of the bicentennial celebration of the French Revolution (Viola: Nobuko Imai, Kent Nagano conducting the Orchestre de Paris). After the concert, Takemitsu sees Olivier Messiaen for the last time.

1990 (60)   Attends numerous events around the world that celebrate his 60th birthday.
March: Premiere of *Visions* commissioned by the Chicago Symphony Orchestra in commemoration of their centennial (Daniel Barenboim conducting the Chicago Symphony).
June: Awarded an honorary doctorate from the University of Leeds, England, and becomes the theme composer at the Leeds Festival.
July: Awarded an honorary doctorate from the University of Durham at the Festival d'Avignon in France. Travels around the south of France with Asaka.

October: Premiere of *From me flows what you call Time*, commissioned by Carnegie Hall to commemorate their 100th anniversary. (Percussion: Nexus, Seiji Ozawa conducting the Boston Symphony Orchestra).
December: Awarded le Prix International Maurice Ravel.

1991 (61) **October**: *Fantasma/Cantos* selected as a representative piece for the "1791-1891-1991" concert of the Vienna Philharmonic. (Clarinet: Richard Stoltzman, Rafael Frühbeck de Burgos conducting the Vienna Philharmonic.)
The Barbican Center in London organizes "Takemitsu Signature."

1992 (62) **May**: *Music Today* festival ends after twenty years.
September: Premiere of *Ceremonial—An Autumn Ode*, commissioned for the opening of the Saitō Kinen Festival Matsumoto (shō: Mayumi Miyata, Seiji Ozawa conducting the Saitō Kinen Orchestra).

1993 (63) **June**: Featured composer at the *Aldeburgh Festival*. Oliver Knussen, conducting the London Sinfonietta, premieres *Archipelago S.* at the festival.
July: Participates as Artistic Director for the projected theater complex at Tōkyō Opera City.
September: Premiere of *Between Tides* commissioned by the Berliner Festspiele.

1994 (64) **April**: Release of the documentary film *Music for the Movies: Tōru Takemitsu* directed by Charlotte Zwerin and produced by Peter Grilli.
October: Receives University of Louisville Grawemeyer Award for *Fantasma/Cantos*.
December: Film score for *Rising Sun*, directed by Philip Kaufman, Takemitsu's first film score for Hollywood.

1995 (65) **March**: Featured composer at the 1st *CineMusic Festival*, in Gstaad Switzerland. Meets David Raksin at the festival.
April: Premiere of *Family Tree*, commissioned by New York Philharmonic to commemorate their 150th anniversary.
Diagnosed with colon cancer and is hospitalized. While in the hospital, writes a journal with cooking recipes and illustrations.
October: Discharged from the hospital recuperates in Miyota. Composes *In the Woods* and *Air*.

November: Release of pop song CD *Tsubasa* ('Wings') sung by pop singer Seri Ishikawa.

1996   **January**: Re-hospitalized.
29th: Attends a party for Tōkyō Opera City Cultural Foundation; returns to hospital.
February 6th: Notified that he is to be awarded the Glenn Gould Prize.
18th: During a snowy day, listens alone to the *St. Matthew Passion* on the radio.
20th: Passes away at 1:15 pm in Toranomon Hospital.
Dies of acute pulmonary edema caused by collagen disease.

©Mitsuko Ono

Afterword

It has been more than ten years since Tōru passed away and, unexpectedly, musicians throughout the world have continued to perform his music. When I listen to these fresh and lively performances, by young musicians whom Takemitsu has never met, I wish Tōru could be here to listen to them too.

In my view, a composer's music speaks for itself, and it is not necessary to talk about their personal life. But when Shōgakukan began this project to compile Takemitsu's works, I started sorting Takemitsu's old materials with the editors and, through this process, became more and more interested in rummaging around and investigating the past. Still, my goal for these interviews was not to talk about the music itself, only about Takemitsu as an individual. But strangely, as it was difficult to talk about Tōru *because* I was so close to him, the interviews became a path to look back on my own life as well.

I was just a normal housewife, but because I was by the side of a composer, I was given an abundant gift called 'music,' and I feel fortunate to have met so many wonderful people through Tōru. In the early stage of our life together, when we were poor and everything was so scarce, there were many important encounters. The sky I gazed up at, through the ashes of war, was so deep and blue. Today I cherish these memories of our youth, when we were released from all manner of constraints, not knowing our path, but still able to live our dream ardently and passionately. Tōru was poor and weak in health, but many people supported him and assisted him, and because of this he was able to focus on his music. So in the end, I think he had a very fortunate life. Nowadays, it is easy to spend our days in idleness, but I miss the passionate energy that surrounded our youth.

Owing to Mr. O'hara's skillful questioning in these interviews, I made several unintended revelations concerning my own personal trivia. If I have inadvertently said something rude concerning anyone, I ask for your forgiveness. And I would also like to thank, from the bottom of my heart, those who have supported us through the years with their unwavering kindness and devotion. Thank you so much.

January 2006

Asaka Takemitsu

Index

CPSIA information can be obtained
at www.ICGtesting.com
Printed in the USA
FSHW021501230120
66401FS